D0088920

Fine 10¢/day. May renew twice, by phone or in person. Charged price + $3 if not returned by semester end.

Fast-Growth Management

Fast-Growth Management

How to Improve Profits with Entrepreneurial Strategies

MACK HANAN

amacom

A Division of American Management Associations

Library of Congress Cataloging in Publication Data

Hanan, Mack.
    Fast-growth management.

    Includes index.
    1. Management. 2. Entrepreneur. I. Title.
HD31.H3124   658.1'554   79-18344
ISBN 0-8144-5559-X

First Printing

To Ben Reiss,
the classic entrepreneur.

He practiced growth the way
    a virtuoso practices his instrument:
With a concentration that denies
    distraction; with a fervor that
Dispels dilution; and with an obsession
    that the entire world – except for
Me, his consultant – was a conspiracy
    to enmesh him in expenses
That would negate his growth.

He kept me separate and apart
    from that complicity
Because I added a little something more
    to his profit
Than I did to his cost.

Preface

In the business climate of the 1980s, either we learn how to grow fast or we will be caught.

Entrepreneurs grow businesses fast; corporate managers are far less successful. At first glance this seems paradoxical. Corporate managers are resource-rich. They work with a veritable treasurehouse of funds, wise counsel, and sophisticated support services. Entrepreneurs, on the other hand, are usually resource-poor. They scramble for dollars, often sacrificing control of their businesses in exchange for venture capital, and then barter away even more of their ownership to pay for competent counsel. No broad constellation of services supports them. Nonetheless, entrepreneurs build fast-growth businesses while corporate managers fail.

Why should this be so?

We all know the traditional explanations. The entrepreneur succeeds because he must succeed or starve. His counterpart, the "corporateur," is salaried and secure. The entrepreneur is a committed soul, a monastic loner, a monomaniac in single-minded pursuit of his objective. The corporateur is selected by scientific screening processes to be a more balanced person, more diversified in his cares and concerns, and a more highly socialized member of a corporate family. The entrepreneur is by definition a risk maximizer. The corporateur minimizes risk; corporate careers are often the reward for survival, not for overwhelming accomplishment. Survival is often earned not by aggressive growth but by opening the doors every morning on time and doing a little bit better with a business today than yesterday.

The distinctions between entrepreneurs and corporateurs are all gross generalizations. They are hackneyed stereotypes. Yet they are true. *Entrepreneurs run businesses differently.*

Entrepreneurs run fast. They run lean, practicing skinny management. They concentrate on doing a few things extremely well. As for the rest, they do them well enough or not at all. They go for the essentials and let nothing deter them. They love the building process, moving into unstructured situations and forming them, shaping them into a commercial enterprise. They are movers and shapers.

The few entrepreneurs in the business world operate through a combination of intuition, wit, and a physiological sixth sense which they variously refer to as gut feel or seat-of-the-pants flying. This book is not for them. No book is. They need room, not books. Most of the rest of us need to go by the book; for us, this is the book. It is intended for the men and women who, by choice or the luck of the draw, will be the business growth managers of the 1980 decade or will be responsible for appointing fast-growth managers and acting as their mentors.

The question that we in The Wellspring Group keep asking ourselves is this: "What can we learn from entrepreneurs that corporate managers can apply to running their businesses for faster profit growth?

Many corporate managers say that the answer to this question is "nothing": the personalities, the motivations, the rewards, and the situations are so different that entrepreneurial business-building strategies cannot be projected into the corporation. I disagree. My associates and I have been studying entrepreneurial businesses since the mid-1960s when we began to work with multibillion-dollar multinational corporations to help them create new business ventures. For the most part, corporate venturing has failed. Yet entrepreneurial businesses have succeeded in many of the same fields. Low overhead, corporate managers asserted. Satisfaction with smaller rewards that would never satisfy corporate criteria. Sure, they said, if you want to devote 24 hours a day to it, you can make anything grow.

What was really happening? On the one hand, growth businesses were being put up. On the other hand, their builders were being put down. The acid test came when corporations, unable to grow their own businesses, began to buy out entrepreneurial ventures. More often than not, they ran them into the ground. To some extent, they smothered them in the crib when they allocated overhead burdens, applied centralized controls, and installed slow-growth management styles in fast-growth businesses. But it was more than high overhead that spelled the doom of these ventures. It was low awareness of the skills required to grow a business.

We have sat in as observers studying dozens of case histories of our clients' failure to grow profitable new businesses. We have participated in many others, sanctifying what we know now to be the egregious error of throwing money at problems instead of throwing entrepreneurial management at them. Our failures, far more than our successes, have led us to the conclusion that growth follows certain laws and that, like all laws, these are inexorable in all but the rare instances when the exception proves the rule. A few years ago, one of our clients named them Hanan's laws. They are listed in the Introduction.

By "grow" we mean profit growth. We have no interest in growth for its own sake. We subordinate sales volume, share of market, and the size of a business itself to profit. The best size for a business is however many people, however much capacity, and whatever volume or market share are most conducive to maximizing profit.

The strategies for fast growth that are described in this book are derived from Hanan's laws. Three of them are leadership strategies; four are management strategies, four others are organizing and operating strategies. Taken together, they are helping many corporateurs achieve growth even inside the frequently viscous medium of a large diversified corporation.

Who manages according to these precepts? Many, maybe even most, superior managers: Gordon Levy, who can probably grow any business he gets his hands around; Bill Gerow, who overcame being a good engineer and, as one of the first really good general managers I worked with, set a standard of excellence in performance that has always stayed with me; Bob Katkov, who extends almost daily his tornadic ability to apply growth strategies to a bewildering variety of conglomerated businesses; and Christine Valmy, who came to the United States with the proverbial $25 in her pocket and founded not just a new business but an entirely new industry.

These managers have, of course, made it look easy. So have others — like Charles Gilbert, who had to invent the machinery to make the product before he could invent the product, and then had to invent a business from its inception so he could market the product. But it isn't easy, even though the management, leadership, organizing, and operating strategies for fast growth are obvious to all of us — once we set them down. They are easier to see than to implement. And they are easier to implement than to keep pure and disencumbered by corporate overengineers who would always like to add one more principle to them.

If there is any message that we have learned from entrepreneurial managers, it is this: Stop perfecting the process of management and start perfecting its objectives. Perfect the growth of these objectives — their size, their speed of achievement, and the sureness with which they can be achieved.

That and that alone is what profit making is all about.

In the the process of perfecting growth objectives, is there any one supercritical propensity that all fast-growth managers must share? If there is, it may well be their sense of being pursued by time: of never having enough, of time continually closing in, of time — in the final analysis — being the archenemy of accomplishment. Growth managers always want yesterday back. They want today to never end. Tomorrow is too late.

To grow fast, time is of the essence. Profits exist only in relation to time. The time value of money is its real value, its only value. If there were an old Chinese proverb governing fast growth, it might very well go like this: *Few strategies, much concentration, little time, many profits.*

Mack Hanan

Contents

Introduction

Since the 1960s, corporate managers have been coming to us and asking in a wide variety of ways what is essentially one question: How can we grow? Our answer to this question is Hanan's laws:

1. The only real growth is profit growth. All other forms of growth — company size, product volume, share of market — enlarge cost rather than net worth.

2. Policy is the allocation of assets to maximize profit growth. All other allocations must be deemed to be contrary to policy since they are contrary to growth.

3. People must be managed as growth assets. All other forms of management erode profit. They also erode people.

4. Branded products and services are difficult to create and even more difficult to market. This makes them extremely difficult to be knocked off by competition. All other products are gifts to competition, not goads.

5. The role of marketing is to create perceptions of unique added value in the minds of a market. All other perceptions are either useless or harmful. In other words, they are without added value to the marketer.

6. The most important sensitivity in managing a growth business is customer sensitivity. All other sensitivities that are allowed to compete with it prove that management is insensitive to the market needs that are the source of its growth.

Because we are not accountants, we have rejected the accountants' solution to the problem of profit growth which emphasizes cost reduction and cost elimination. We share their cost sensitivities. But we believe that no company can save its way to salvation. Besides, the key cost is rarely the one you pay today. It is the opportunity cost of tomorrow's revenue source that is missing because you allocated today's investment money to the wrong objective.

Growth requires the infusion of new cash flow. How much? *More.* When is there enough? *Never.* Our concentration is on the cost-effective accumulation of new profits, not cost reduction management. We therefore favor what we call the Wellspring solution, which concentrates on speeding up the rate and size of profit accumulation. We think of it as a business management approach to growing.

Seeking Real-World Secrets of Growth

Given our bias, it was inevitable, then, that we would look for answers to the real world of managers who are successful practitioners of fast growth. How are they managing it? Why is the management of fast growth different from managing marginally incremental growth? We began our search for common denominators. We tried to find basic principles. We become intrigued with the possibility that there may even be secrets of fast growth, known to relatively few managers and practiced with results by even fewer.

The secrets of fast growth: what a discovery! Who would refuse to pay a king's ransom for them? And we would hold them in our hands.

What we came up with had verisimilitude. The secrets seemed right. After all, they had passed the test of experience. They stood up to what we knew. Yet in our work with clients we have never been satisfied to plead solely from experience. Why should we accept less for ourselves? So we tested our entrepreneurial strategies across a fair sampling of industries encompassing consumer products, high technology electronics, and capital-intensive industrial hardware manufacture as well as in service businesses such as communications, transportation, and finance. They still worked.

As we set them down, we came to a humbling realization. Secrets indeed. There were no secrets. Every one of the strategies of entrepreneurial growth management that we had discovered was, in truth, a basic business principle that has been part and parcel of the folklore of the free enterprise system since time began. As schoolchildren, we know most of them before we put up our first lemonade stand. They are recited as a litany by virtually every speech-making business manager. What a trite collection of commercial Americana our strategies turned out to be:

1. Profit is the name of the game.
2. Build a better mousetrap.
3. The customer is always right.
4. Either you run the business or it will run you.
5. People, not organization charts, make businesses.
6. If you want to be successful, make others successful.

Going Back to Basics

Are these truisms the underlying strategies for fast profit growth? Are they what growing a business at a better rate than the gross national product is all about—homilies that offer nothing that is stunning in their novelty, baffling in their complexity, or charismatic in their ingenuity? They are.

Underlying principles are always simple. How could they be otherwise? It is superstructures that are complicated, not foundations. In corporate management we have permitted underlying principles to become obscure. Every now and then, usually on Founder's Day, we recall momentarily that one or another of today's major corporations was originated by an entrepreneurial manager who knew what to concentrate on, what to do well enough, and what to ignore. In spite of the role models provided by Will Durant (the original builder of General Motors), Clarence Francis (who built General Foods), George Eastman (who created Kodak), and Edwin Land of Polaroid, we have been so obsessed with becoming well-rounded managers that we have neglected to become sharply pointed in our principal mission of accelerating the growth of our businesses.

The need is greater now than ever. From above, inflationary pressures knock the tops off our profit curves. From below, nonproductive expenses and spiraling costs drive up our break-even points. Management is the art of what goes on in between.

The Xomox model is a good example of the kind of fast-growth management we advocate – the kind that makes superior profits in spite of being hemmed in by inflation and the cost spiral. Xomox Corporation is a hardware manufacturer. It makes Teflon-sleeve plug valves, a type of valve that is essentially the same in basic form and concept as the lead versions of that product found in the ruins of Pompeii, dating back to 79 A.D. The valve business is a commodity business. Over 300 manufacturers compete for a slice of the same pie. Yet Xomox, a small company, has consistently earned 30 percent average return on equity. How does it manage?

Xomox management has slavishly followed fast-growth business principles. It has concentrated on one product, dedicating itself to making it superior. It has concentrated on selling the product principally to one industry, petrochemicals, where its advantages of moldability into a variety of useful shapes, inertness under corrosive chemical processes, and no need for lubrication combine to create high use value. It has concentrated on providing superior applications engineering services and aggressively marketing their profit-improvement values, not the valves. As a result of its concentration on improving customer profit, Xomox has improved its own.

To grow a business fast, we need to go back to the Xomox brand of basics. We are aware that temptations abound. The lures of running fat, running safe, and running slow are always present, sometimes dangled invitingly by corporate management in much the same way that old-fashioned earth mothers say "Eat!" But they are to be resisted mightily.

In the words of one fast-track manager, "There are always invitations to come to the devil's party. Go ahead, add a few more bodies to staff. How can you build an empire without people? Besides, you can always find something useful for them to do. Don't run so close to capacity. Add on to plant. You'll sleep better at night. Enlarge your market share. Sure, you don't have to be big to be good. But if you're really good, isn't it true that you won't be able to keep from becoming big? No company remains small by choice. There is always somewhere I can relax my growth thrust, forsake my mission, or let up on my principles. But I use temptations as an enemy. I compete against them. They are my toughest competitors. To the extent that I win, I grow."

Applying Dedication to Growing a Business

Turning down invitations to the devil's party takes dedication. What is dedication? It is the most intense form of concentration, which is one of the attributes of genius — according to the testimony of geniuses themselves, the single most important attribute. When Albert Einstein was asked how he came to have a genius for mathematics, he said he didn't. His real talent was music. If he had concentrated on music as completely as he had dedicated himself to mathematics, he felt certain that he would have been a musical genius. Picasso's dedication was to destruction. He said that he painted by selectively removing miscellaneous elements until what remained was his true creation. A painting, he said, was the sum of many destructions.

What Picasso was applying was the 80-20 rule, which says that 20 percent of what you do gives you 80 percent of the results you get. Ray Charles applies the 80-20 rule to music. He travels with only 20 percent of an orchestra, picking up the remaining 80 percent wherever he goes. "The 20 percent I take with me make 80 percent of the music," he says.

Vince Lombardi applied the same rule to football. He ran the same few plays over and over again. They composed about 20 percent of his playbook, but they accounted for 80 percent of his yardage. By concentrating on them, he was able to perfect their execution to the point where no other team could stop them even when they knew they were coming—which was 80 percent of the time.

Growing a business fast is a form of genius; that is, it is a dedication. That is why *think few* is good advice for fast business growers. Concentrate on the essentials. Dedicate yourself to perfecting them and to resisting all attempts to expand their number or complicate their intent. Dedication is the best way to counter the two inherent constraints on growth, time and money.

Dollars are always limited and always run out too soon. Sometimes they can be replenished. But the time constraint cannot be fudged. It is time, not dollars, that will be your ultimate limitation on growth. To grow fast is to manage time as growth's chief resource.

The constraining nature of time is revealed by the fact that other resources are always being traded off for more of it. Added cost is incurred to gain time. Effectiveness is traded off to save time. Short-term results are traded for longer-term benefits and improvements. Low earnings, no dividends, and negative cash flow in the present time are the price for growth profits, or at least the promise of them, later on. Short-term profits are hostages to considerations of time. They are always on the trading block.

Yet there is no substitute for them. Time itself has money value. Indeed, time *is* money. Money is also a factor of time. The present value of future revenues often determines how worthwhile they will be. Opportunity cost, the loss of future earnings, often determines how worthwhile another investment will appear to be.

The time constraint is the principal source of risk. Without time pressure—with elastic time frames within which you could compare stakes to resources and create endless options to optimize their ratio—management would be a pastime . . . literally, something with which to pass time.

There are two principal risks that you can take with your resources. One is the risk of not accelerating growth. What is risked here is the shelf life of your resources. How long will they remain fresh, highly motivational, and competitively superior? How long will opportunity last? These are time considerations. The second risk is to take the fast track to growth in a few selected areas of your business.

Choosing the fast-growth areas with care, and planning with skill the strategies to achieve growth objectives, avoids the problem of catastrophic failure. Survival of the enterprise is not at stake. The corporation is not being bet. Instead, you can concentrate on bringing home a few new winners, not avoiding losers. Many entrepreneurial managers fortify their winner orientation by following two principles. One is risk minimizing, sometimes known as thinking small. The other is risk division.

Risk minimizing in a growing business is a question of magnitude. Suppose you have the chance to invest $10 million in a growth opportunity. There is a fifty-fifty risk of making $50 million. This is the best case. There is a much lower risk of making $30 million and an even lower risk of making $20 million. The odds are probably stacked against making $50 million. The chance of success may be only 25 percent. The best risk is for the worst case, the smallest reward. Risk-justified growth usually lies somewhere in between as the most likely case.

You can practice risk division in two ways while you accelerate growth. One is by dividing big risks into smaller bites. The other is by composing a strategy mix of higher and lower risks. If a total budget at risk were $10 million, with a 10 percent chance of failure to achieve accelerated growth and a 90 percent chance of making $50 million, it would be prudent risk management to invest $15 million to the first go, no-go point. This decision might be based on an 80 percent expectation of success. If a go decision is made at the $15 million point, you could have a 90 percent expectation of success. Now you can invest $25 million. What happens if a competitor gets in first? You may be left with a $35 million business instead of one worth $50 million. You still have a winner.

Think liberally but move conservatively when money is on the line. If there is any secret to successful growth acceleration, this is it. The key word is *move*. Apart from estimating the odds, the main growth strategy is the willingness to move. That is what being an entrepreneurial manager is all about.

The strategies to move on are what fast-growth management is all about.

Adequate vs. Superior Management

Is there an alternative to fast growth? If a business is capable of being fast-grown, the alternative is adequate management. It is the kind of management that most managers are taught and that an increasing number of managers are being fired for. An illustrative scenario occurred a while ago when the president of a multimillion-dollar division was invited by his parent company's directors to resign. He protested. "I brought the company through the recession. One of our competitors failed. Another was saved only by being acquired. I've showed a profit every year since then. Our competitors have been content to break even or limit their losses. In one of our key markets, I am even increasing our penetration. Call it what you will; at worst, I call it adequate management."

"So do we," the directors said.

"Then what is the problem?" the president asked.

"The problem is that adequate is no longer adequate."

"If adequate is no longer adequate," the president asked, "what is it?"

"Adequate is inadequate," the directors said.

"What then is adequate?"

"Superior."

"And what is superior?" the president asked.

"Aha!" said the directors. "We thought you didn't know."

This is not to say that we believe there is no place for adequate managers. There is. It is with our competitors. For ourselves and for our clients, we look for the ability to run up the growth of a business at a fast rate. That is superior management. Without fast growth as the standard of performance, seemingly unstoppable rises in taxes, inflation, and nonproductive costs superimposed on enlarged operating costs will act to reduce narrow margins even further. The chance to generate the capital needed for corporate growth will diminish.

Fast-growth managers are the last-ditch capitalists of the final quarter of the twentieth century. They are the creators of corporate wealth. The strategies they employ are the modern version of the means of production: the tools, the skills, and the styles that take the potential in a business for swift profit making and turn it into the reality of significant new earnings.

Growing and Turning Around: Blood Brothers

It is noteworthy, but not at all strange, that the ground rules for turning a business around are remarkably similar to some of the guidelines for fast growth. When turnaround managers take hold of a declining business, one of the first things they do is to locate its winners and put them in one pile. The turned-around business will be rebuilt around them. The next step is to identify the losers. They go into another pile for weeding out, either by sale or by dissolution.

Going further, turnaround managers break out the winning businesses into profit centers which are related to discrete markets. They run them lean and tight. Payroll and overhead are slashed to the bone. Each manager wears a variety of hats throughout every business day. But, principally, he is a money manager. His chief function is to allocate extremely well-controlled assets for high-multiple results — in other words, for fast growth.

Once a falling business has been stabilized, it becomes a prime candidate for fast-growth management. It has been thinned down, much like an entrepreneurial start-up. It needs a major inflow of cash. It stands in a more harmonious relation to its resources, especially its sources of funds; namely, the customers in its core markets who will perceive the greatest value in doing business with it. Now it must sell.

The fundamental pointers toward growth are the same whether you are starting a new business from scratch, turning around a diminishing business, or simply taking a profitable enterprise that is in a slow-growth or no-growth mode and putting the heat on it. This suggests that growth has rules; it does. It suggests that growth can be based on a variety of business situations: those that are new, those that are going nowhere fast, and those that are going down the tube; it can. It suggests that the management of growth businesses is a discipline which men and women can apply across the broad band of profit-making industrial environments—and even those that are not for profit; they can.

Some management thinkers have expressed the belief that the chief commitment to growing a business fast is to think small. By this they mean to keep the cost base down. But this is only half the growth equation. What about profit? Every fast-growth manager must think big about it. Otherwise he will have a small business with a bottom line to match. The best equation reads like this: *Think small about your investment— think large about your return on it.*

PART I

The Five Fast-Growth Guidelines

1

Get Your Act Together — Growth Begins in Your Head

Markets, we believe, are the source of growth funds. You cannot grow your own business unless you contribute to the growth of your key customers. But what is the originating *source of growth?* Growth must begin in a manager's head — your head — or it will begin nowhere. You must be the apostle of growth for your business: its spokesman, its symbol, its policy maker. Your head must be home base for the motivation to grow, the lair of the growth tiger that will stalk the halls of your organization day in and day out in search of superior profits.

What do you have to do to get your growth act together? You cannot be a potential growth manager; you must be actual. You cannot be what James Thurber once called a fractional impactionist; you must hit your growth objectives squarely on the nose, not merely brush against them. You cannot delegate growth; you must manage its production yourself. How can you deliver?

Five guidelines will help. If you follow them, they will steer you to king-size opportunities, encourage you to strike while the irons are hot and not wait for the perfect moment, help you keep faith in your own game plan, insure your concentration on finding ways into your markets without losing sight of your cut-out points, and reassure you that the near-total dedication required to grow a business fast is worth the personal cost.

1. Fish for Whales—Screen Out Minnows

Fast growth comes from catching big fish. This means selling big-winner products to heavy profit-contributor markets at premium prices. Little winners won't make it. Neither will cultivating low profit contributors. Prices that are less than premium will delay the onset of growth or prevent it entirely.

It is relatively easy to start out on a growth mission filled with the commitment to pursue only whales – the main-chance type of opportunity. Yet there is a disease entity that regularly afflicts growth managers when they hit the wall – that is, when they encounter the first resistance to their objectives. The disease is called growth frenzy. Its main symptom is that a manager will do anything to grow the business. This is the time when whale hunting may be forsaken for going after minnows with the rationale that any sale is a good sale and every dollar counts.

At the precise moment that the whaler's harpoon is set aside for the minnow fisherman's bent safety pin, the growth mission ends. Business as usual sets in. Once that happens, it is all but impossible to reverse the trend. Nothing is ever the same again. The product may have been depositioned from its pre-eminence as the perceived value leader. Its price may have been lowered from premium levels. Its market base may have been broadened to include lower profit contributors. Maximum profit per unit will have been sacrificed for volume – the traditional anvil on which commodity product margins are regularly hammered flat.

What kind of mental set is required to go on with the search for whales if the initial pickings are slim?

The best response is not frenzy but a reassessment of your going-in assumptions. What did you originally assume that is turning out not to be true? Did you assume you had the facts about your most probable market segment – their needs, their predispositions to buy, their value-to-price ratio? It may be that your facts are not facts at all but incorrect assumptions. Your fact-finding methods may be at fault. Your interpretations may be overoptimistic. A key piece of information may be missing entirely.

Did you assume you had the facts about your most probable customers' major costs that you can reduce or eliminate? Or did you assume you knew their most attractive sales revenue opportunities? It may be that their priorities are not what you assume them to be.

Did you make assumptions about the most acceptable channels of distribution, about the timing and nature of expected competitive response, about the comfort level of customer decision makers in becoming educated to your offering if it is new, about dislocations you may be threatening unknowingly in one part of a customer operation while you are smoothing out another, or about the minimum introductory weight of advertising required to create a sufficiently high "blood level" of customer awareness and positive attitudes?

If growth is not being generated according to your plan, one thing is certain: At least one of your assumptions is wrong. You must find it and correct it, quickly but coolly. Errant assumptions are always at the root of failure to achieve planned growth. Sometimes the corrected assumptions, when they are made, will negate your growth plan. In that case you will have to replan; to go back to the drawing board. This is generally an embarrassment. It is also a lot of work. But when you consider the alternative—folding the business as a fast-growth candidate—it is not quite so bad.

So remember this rule of thumb. If you find yourself deviating from whaling to minnowing, take it as a portent that your assumptions are out of whack with the real-world environment of your markets. Fast growth is endangered. Find a basis for returning to whale fishing, which is the only place that growth profits can be found, or get out of the water.

2. Move Fast After Your Homework—Waiting Is Destructive

A business growth plan is a hot property. It is temporal, transient, very much oriented to today and tomorrow, not the figurative someday. Every growth plan should bear the label "Strike while hot." In growing a business fast, procrastination is not only the thief of time; it can also be the destroyer of opportunity.

In the entrepreneurial world, the thrust among self-dependent business builders is to do everything "yesterday." Today is late, tomorrow is too late. Besides, tomorrow never comes. Profits today can exceed the value of profits tomorrow even if later profits will be greater. If today's lesser profits are put to work properly, they can exceed tomorrow's. At the same time, they relieve the manager of the need to wait to grow the business.

All the while, the entrepreneur is thinking: Imagine if we had had the money yesterday.

Business growers know the time value of money. Double-digit inflation is only one reason. Opportunity cost is the chief culprit. It is not just the accumulation of fast-grown dollars you have to be concerned about. It is what the dollars can do to make more dollars by being invested back into the business. Yes, managers of growth businesses make money. But when it comes right down to it, it is the money they make that really makes the money. This is the basic reason why growing businesses tend to continue to grow. They have the money.

Every business growth opportunity has two kinds of cost associated with it. The first is the expense involved in financing a strategic decision. No matter how much money is involved, this cost is almost always affordable. The second cost is the lost revenues that could have been earned if the same amount of money had been invested in other strategies. If the amount lost is larger than what is actually brought in, it is never affordable.

The specter of unaffordable opportunity cost haunts every growth manager. "How should I be doing what I'm doing?" is only one part of the dilemma. The other is, "Should I be doing something else?"

How can you take the fullest measure of precaution against the answer's being yes—but coming so late that the question becomes an ex post facto "Should I *have been doing* something else?" The best way, perhaps the only way, is to do your homework and then move to start the growth process. The longer you wait, the greater your risk.

When is your homework really finished? When is it done well enough that you can begin to act on it by making the first serious commitment of your limited, hard-won resources? In truth, the time is never. There is no such thing as enough facts. If you wait for that magic moment, you will never act. This is exactly what happens to many would-be corporateurs. They have been supported for so long by the accumulated fact base of the slow-growth or no-growth mature business that they cannot wean themselves away. Facts become their security blanket. While they massage facts, their opportunity grows away from them.

If you cannot have enough information, what can you have? Like it or not, you will have to settle for less than everything you always wanted to know but as much as you can find out before the whistle blows. Strangely enough, while this is not enough, it will generally be sufficient if you use fair assumptions to fill the gap between what you know and what you would like to know. If you make fair assumptions—not necessarily excellent ones—these will generally turn out to be what you would like to know.

Entrepreneurs are said to operate from interior knowledge. They know the facts about what their markets need, what they will prefer as the preeminent benefit for their needs, and how much of a premium price they are willing to pay to possess it. This interior knowledge, so called because it does not depend on any formal market research, is known as intuition. "He is an intuitive businessman," we say. And what is intuition? It is the ability to make fair assumptions.

It is a truism that the better the fact base, the fairer the assumptions that can be made to supplement it. What this says is that the narrower the gap between what you know and what you would like to know, the easier it is to fill it accurately. No one can argue against that. So the recommendation to move fast is actually a recommendation to do just enough homework so your assumptions will be fair enough for you to allocate assets and activate your plan.

What kinds of things are you most likely going to have to

assume? They will be the future impacts of all the factors in your business situation that you cannot control. Where will the economy be in six months? In twelve? Make a fair assumption. Base it on facts about where the economy has been, where it seems to be going, and what forces may work on it to propel it there or impede it. What laws affecting your business will the Congress pass? Make a fair assumption. Base it on facts about the present composition of the legislature, the most probable corrective effects of impending elections, and the likelihood of presidential support or vetoes. Do the same with the other situational factors.

Getting facts is difficult. Making assumptions is even more so. To get facts, you have to work hard. To make fair assumptions, you have to think hard. How do you think assumptively? You think probabilistically because assumptions are probabilities. If you are not familiar with the assumptive thought process, the following sample dialog between a growth manager and his consultant will show you how to do it in your head.

Consultant: Are you planning on an economic recession over the three-year time frame of your plan?

Manager: How can I know?

Consultant: Oh, you already know. You just don't know you know. Let me help you reveal your knowledge to yourself. Suppose we say there is a 100 percent chance that there will be a recession. Let's factor it into your plan.

Manager: That's ridiculous. A 100 percent chance would make it a sure thing. It's not.

Consultant: All right, then. Let's say there's no chance at all for a recession. How's that?

Manager: Just as ridiculous. That makes it a sure thing too. I'd say there's at least a 40 percent chance for a recession at the minimum.

Consultant: What about the maximum?

Manager: No better than 60 or 70 percent at most. Let's split the difference and say 66²/₃ percent.

Consultant: In other words, you're assuming that the chance for recession lies between 40 percent and 66²/₃ percent. That averages out to a better than 50 percent chance that your growth will be affected by an economic downturn.

Manager: But how do you know?

Consultant: I don't. You do.

Manager: How do you know that I know?

Consultant: I don't. You told me.

A good rule to follow is to assume you know. Then try to bring your assumption to the surface in dialog with yourself or a never-say-die devil's advocate on the basis of probabilities. When you have fine-tuned them to the point where you know what you think, move on them fast.

3. Play Your Own Game—Otherwise Why Plan?

Your business growth plan is your growth game. While your market is your most precious resource, the plan is your single most important tool for committing that resource to work as a contributor of growth profits. Managers of slow-growth or no-growth businesses think of their plans as a means of putting their own people to work: of gainfully employing them and their allied resources. But if you are committed to fast growth, you must regard your plan as the machine that will mobilize your market as a heavy contributor of profits to your business.

A growth plan is a market's working papers. We say that it positions the market as well as your business because it contains the market's *position description*—in other words, it presumes what the market will do (buy), how much it will do it (volume), when it will do it (time frame), under what control (marketing strategy pressure), and for what reward (perceived value).

Businesses grow because they are able to put their markets to work buying from them, using and using up the values they buy, and then buying more. Market share is a measure of market work. Turnover is a measure of market energy. Profits are a measure of market motivation to possess value. They are an index of market reward just as surely as they provide the criteria of your own reward.

If you cannot get a market to go to work for you and put out —that is, expend in your behalf—you will not grow. As a growth manager, you should think of yourself as your market's employer. This makes you a manager of their assets; in effect, their money manager. Your business growth plan is actually a money management plan for converting your market's investment of work on your behalf into an even greater return. There are four ways to do this: seize your plan's situation, quantify its objectives, frame the objectives for three years, and mix its strategies.

SEIZE YOUR PLAN'S SITUATION

Given the importance of your plan to your growth, you can understand why your plan must be treated with respect. How do you respect a business plan ? You implement it. Since it is your game, play it. To the extent that you ignore it or deviate from it without cause, you treat your plan with disrespect.

Your original plan will reflect what is known as your business situation. This is the sum total of the impact being made on your ability to market by the variable factors outside your management control. What are they? The five major factors in every business situation are economic changes that can slow down or speed up your sales, technological innovations that can preempt your product's benefits, legislation that can add to your costs or clamp down on your sales, market demand swings toward or away from your product or product category, and competitive actions that can undermine the perception your markets have of your product's value. Once you take these factors into consideration in formulating your growth plan, implement it quickly before one or more of them undergoes significant change. You can be certain of one thing: They will.

As soon as any factor in your situation changes, account for its new impact on your plan's objectives and strategies. Then implement your plan quickly before other factors can change.

It is sound management practice to think of your plan as a hot property. Any significant change in your business situation can cool it off fast. So you should put it into action before it loses the fiery heat of immediacy. A cold plan is dead. It has lost its relevance, superseded by change. When that happens, a new, changed situation deserves your respect. You can acknowledge the change by incorporating it into the operating base of a revised growth plan.

QUANTIFY YOUR PLAN'S OBJECTIVES

What does a business growth plan look like? Exhibit 1 shows a growth plan's highlights. There are three principal sections. The plan leads off with the growth objectives of the business. They set its course by answering the question, "Where is this business going?" Growth objectives are always presented in numbers. They are always quantified. There are no fuzzy declarations such as a general promise "to grow the business" and no weasels, hedges, or cop-outs such as "to dominate our industry," or "to take leadership," or "to gain the largest market share." None of these is an objective. All are hopes. Some are prayers.

Your growth objectives begin with what you plan to take to the bank. This will be net profit after taxes, the be-all and end-all of growth and therefore its ultimate objective. Nothing must be allowed to surpass it in prominence as the driving force of the business. Return on investment is the best measure of the cost-effectiveness with which the net profit is being made. It can tell how good a growth manager you are. How should you regard sales and profits? Sales volume expressed as numbers of units and as dollars can reveal your marketing productivity. A high profit figure that is contributed by relatively few units may speak for a high productivity of marketing in gaining user acceptance of a premium price per unit. The converse is also true.

Fast growth and high marketing productivity are directly related. Each of them, in fact, may be defined in terms of the other. Fast growth is the end result of productive marketing. High marketing productivity is the principal leverage on fast growth.

In the growth objectives section of your plan, the totals tell

Exhibit 1. Business growth plan.

1. **Growth objectives**

   (by most likely case/worst case)

   1.1. Total net profit

   1.1.1. Increment vs. year ago

   1.2. Return on investment (%)

   1.2.1. Increment vs. year ago

   1.3. Total gross sales volume (#)

   1.3.1. Increment vs. year ago

   1.4. Total gross sales volume ($)

   1.4.1. Increment vs. year ago

2. **Strategy mixes to achieve growth objectives**

   (by market segment)

   2.1. Segment (SIC# _____)*

   Profit contribution ($ ÷ %)

   Sales contribution (# ÷ $ ÷ %)

   2.1.1. Product/service systems to be sold

   Total investment required ($)

   Individual investment required ($)

   2.1.2. Promotion systems to move the product/service systems

   Total investment required ($)

   Individual investment required by:

   2.1.2.1. Sales and distribution strategy

   2.1.2.2. Advertising support strategy

   2.1.2.3. Sales promotion strategy

   2.1.3. Premium pricing strategy by individual product/ service system

   2.2. Segment (SIC# _____)

   (Repeat as in 2.1., above.)

3. **Controls to monitor progressive achievement of growth objectives**

   3.1. Methods and milestones at which to measure growth

   3.2. Methods and milestones at which to measure changes in market needs and preferences for benefit values

*Standard Industrial Classification

you how much you have grown. The incremental gain over a year ago tells you how much you are growing. As a growth manager, you should be evaluated on current increments, not on past increments, not on the total profit on sales volume of the business—which, after all, represents past growth—but on what you have done lately and what you expect to do in the near-term future. Not only should growth managers be judged on their ability to maximize incremental gain. They themselves, as managers, should be regarded by their top managements as increments: incremental profit contributors if they produce, incremental costs if they do not.

Fast-growth management is best thought of, therefore, as if it were called maximum-increment management. If you think of it this way, you will never deceive yourself about your mission. You are not growing organizations, you are not growing markets, and you are not growing product franchises as much as you are growing marginal contributions of profit.

FRAME YOUR PLAN'S THREE-YEAR OBJECTIVES

Until the recession that ended in 1975, rolling out ten-year projections of objectives was a popular hobby among business growers. Some of them even got away with it. What made it possible was their business situation. Unlike today's, it could often be reasonably well predicted. That is past history now. No one can see ten years ahead economically, technologically, legislatively, socially, or competitively. Even a five-year projection is a myth, although less so than trying to foresee a decade. The value of five-year objectives is that thinking through the fourth and fifth years can help rationalize the third-year projection. That is really as far as you need to go. A fair rule is that if you cannot achieve faster than average growth in three years, budgeting for two more years is probably throwing good investment money after bad.

Even if your managers or their directors, shareowners, or other financiers were willing to let you try another go-round, any market that would permit it would probably not be a growth culture. If it were, a competitive tiger would have run you out.

All things considered—the increasing thinness of your assumptions as you go further ahead into time coupled with the increasing richness of the investment base of patience money that you require—a three-year projection of objectives is far enough. If you need the disciplinary effect of years four and five to tighten year three, fine. That is the best and perhaps the sole justification for rolling out a five-year pro forma.

Within your three-year plan you should have two sets of numbers for each objective. One set will display the most likely case you can make. This will be your realistic forecast of growth, revealing the objectives you actually expect to reach. If you had to, you could sign your name in blood against them. A second set of numbers will be your worst case. These are critically important.

Worst-case objectives are your bottom-most bottom line, the floor below which your growth cannot and will not fall. They represent your minimal growth. They are not most likely. Your bet is that they are in fact unlikely. But you must admit that they are possible.

What is the value of worst-case objectives since no one wants to achieve them? No business deserves to be called a fast-growth business unless its worst-case objectives also represent faster-than-average growth. Therein lies their value. They signal to you what kind of business you really have on your hands. At the worst it will grow fast. Most likely it will grow faster.

If your worst-case objectives project slow growth or no growth, you may not have a genuine fast-growth business. The service they perform is akin to flashing a red light in your eyes. They urge you to stop, look, and listen to your fact base: Does it really contain the facts? What about your assumptions? How much flab is in them based on what you prefer them to be rather than what a more hard-nosed audit would reveal them to be? You can always fool yourself for a while about whether you have a growth business. But you cannot fool anyone else for very long after. That is why your worst-case objectives are vital to you.

What makes a set of objectives into a worst case? All that it takes is a scenario that is really not very much different from the most likely case. Sometimes only one major change in your most likely scenario will transform it into a worst case. Market penetration into a new customer segment may be delayed, for example. Or a new product may not take off in time. The imposition of a legislated nonproductive cost may be advanced, a tax relief may be delayed, or a competitor may turn out to be bolder, luckier, or smarter than you had any reason to believe. The gross number of events is usually small. But they are the kind of events that carry a large impact on cash flow. Sometimes, of course, the bottom drops out. Everything goes wrong. What results is the worst case. But this is not most likely.

MIX THREE STRATEGIES IN YOUR PLAN

What is the prime purpose of a growth plan? The plan exists to help you formulate and declare your objectives. The objectives *are* the plan. What is the purpose of objectives? One answer is that they impose on you the most cost-effective strategy mix with which to achieve them. Objectives precondition strategies. By keeping your objectives clearly in mind, you can help insure that your strategies will be the most effective mix to deliver your growth. At the same time, they will be the least costly. If they become costlier than they need to be, or less efficient, your strategies will detract from your objectives, not accomplish them.

As Exhibit 1 shows, strategies make sense only when they are market-centered—that is, when they are custom-tailored to each specific market segment you serve. In this way, they can match up with market needs and values. In this way, too, you will be able to know the contribution that each market segment is making to your growth and the investment in strategic marketing that is required to yield it.

You have three fundamental strategies to mix and match on a per market basis. One is the products and services you select to sell to each market. The second is the promotional system that will move your products at growth rates. The third is your premium pricing strategy. For each market, what premium penetration price will you choose for entry? When, under what circumstances, and by how much will you take it down yet still maintain it at a premium level? The answers are so interwoven with your product and promotional system plans that you must deal with all three at once. After all, your market will be doing the same thing.

Finally, the business growth plan outline asks for the controls you will apply to monitor the achievement of your objectives. How and when will you measure your incremental growth? How and when will you go into your heaviest profit-contributing markets and measure the persistence of or change in their needs and preferences for values? These two controls will tell you if you have been on course and if you can continue to expect to be.

4. Be a Workaholic—How Else Will You Get It Done?

There is no easy way to grow a business fast. A growth business is not a full-time occupation. It is really two full-time occupations in one: a day job and an evening job, a weekday career and a weekend career. It is not so much something that you are in. It is something that is in you. It is harder than any work, more fun than play, and an addictive involvement second to none in its intensity.

Only addicts need apply. Growth is the prize of men and women who are driven by an inner compulsion to grasp the tail of an alligator. Be advised: Once you grasp the alligator's tail, there's no way to let go. The moot question always is, do you have the alligator or does the alligator have you?

Successful growth managers are had by their alligators. They care for them and feed them during virtually every waking hour. They dream about them at night. They bring them home with them and take them on vacations. They become boon companions, one and inseparable. If you wanted to start up your own business and you stood before a venture capitalist professing any lesser dedication to your alligator, you would not get the money. Nor should you. The same dedication should apply to corporate growth ventures.

Growth, the addiction to fast profit making, solicits managers who work without thinking of what they do as work. For them, growing a business is not what they are required to do. That would make it work. Growing a business is, instead, what they want to do more than anything else. That makes it a mission.

Missionaries work their missions the way miners work their mines: without surcease. There is no other way. How else will they get it done? No one will do it for them. Many factors seem to conspire against them. Few outsiders who have not heard their call understand them. Business builders are termed selfish by the outside world. They go on. They are called insensitive to other values, isolated in their own little worlds, consumed by their own lust and greed. They go on. They are admired, feared, disliked, sometimes revered, often reviled, but they appear impervious to scorn and praise alike. They go on.

The issue is not whether their work ethic should be praised as a virtue or condemned as a vice. It is simply a necessity, to be included without pride or prejudice in the checklist of minimum daily requirements to boost a business faster than the norm.

In the semantics of our time, it is fashionable to give practitioners of the work ethic the name workaholics as an acknowledgment of their inner drive. A better word is *concentrators* on a single objective. It is not necessarily extraordinary intelligence, blinding flashes of insight, or a rare ability to put structure around an unstructured situation that makes a growth manager. It is the talent to rivet attention, to fixate, to shut out all temptations to be diverted or distracted or to have a single-minded purpose denatured.

What kind of correlate can you compare it with? It is somewhat like being in love but without the blinders that love imposes. In business you must be able to see the warts. But you must be no less addicted.

How can you comfort yourself in the throes of your addiction? Your mission is transcendent. You are not merely working; you are building a fast growth business. And how will you get others less addicted to follow you? By leading them in fast growth, gathering them up in the mission of catching the curve.

5. Make It Your Job to Penetrate—Then Hand Off to a Custodian

Market penetration is the cutting edge of business growth. To be a business grower, you must be a fast penetrator who is able to get deep into a market's values, identify product or service benefits that will add significantly to them, and command a premium price for their delivery.

Penetration is one of the true arts of business management. Penetrators are rare birds. There are never very many of them, a fact which is attested to, at least in part, by the small number of new product introductions and new business developments that succeed. There are of course other true management arts. Conservators are also scarce, representing an unequal distribution of the talent to hold back the inevitable decline of a mature business by conserving its market position as long as possible. In a sense, they represent the skill of holding back competitive penetrators.

Managers who can turn losing businesses around, stopping their cash outflow, stabilizing them, and then starting them up again are not abundant but they are not as rare as penetrators or conservators. They have at least two things in their favor. Unlike conservators, they do not have a going concern to be considered. Theirs is going down, not going on. They can practice remedial management more radically. And unlike penetrators, turnarounders have an established business to work with. It may not be much. But it is often better than starting from scratch because there is at least one less unknown—what will not work has been painfully learned.

That leaves the custodians, the managers of slow-growth or no-growth businesses. They are in greatest supply because they are in greatest demand; most businesses are custodial in nature. They are the 80 percent of all managers who yield no more than 20 percent of all profits. While custody of a business is more method than art, you should make friends with custodial managers because they will inherit your business after your penetration has been made. This is the only cost-effective way to run an enterprise.

Your role as a business grower is to penetrate up to a point. The point can be defined in several ways but it is always at the same place: the point where the slope of your penetration curve begins to slacken so that each successive unit of sale returns a diminished profit. You can think of this point as representing a moment in time, a percentage of market share, an amount of sales volume or dollars of profit. It is a point of diminishing returns for profit. It is also a point of increasing unit costs. The business is a commodity. However you regard it, the signal is clear. You have done your job.

How do you know? When you have achieved fast penetration, you will have maximized the contribution your business can make — not finalized it, because there will still be profits to be made. But you will have managed the major part of its yield. Think of this as your job, being a majority manager. From then on, the minority of profits per unit of time will flow from your business. They will still grow but they will grow slower. Fast growth will have come to an end.

There are valid reasons why this will be so. Premium price will soften. Sensitivity to its margin will increase. Direct competitors will challenge your franchise, using your own technology. Indirect technologies may also become competitive. Your market's growth will slow or the rate of growth of your slice of it will peter out. Cost of sales will rise. Your gut feel will tell you if nothing else will: Your business has become mature. What is a penetrator doing in a mature business? The fun of fast growth will have gone with the profit. Increasing restlessness will have taken its place.

Penetrators are too valuable to be employed in any activity but penetrative growth. As you move your business up the growth curve, keep your hand on it. When you feel the knee of the curve approaching — the place where the rate of growth slows and the curve flattens to a plateau — begin to release your grasp. This is the optimal time to seek redeployment. It is the optimal time to hand off your business to a custodial manager who will smooth out its remaining profit-making capability over an extended time frame. His thrust will be slower paced. Time extension, not compression, will key his pressure on the business. Maintaining a market, not generating it, will be his strategic kingpin. Relaxing premium price reluctantly, not pegging it high and commanding it, will be his means of making money.

This is a vastly different schedule of professional qualities. It requires a distinct mix of skills all its own, personal characteristics that emphasize patience, a fascination with short strokes and fine tuning, and a mind set totally foreign to your own. You may not want to be such a manager. You may even wonder how such managers come to be. But they are vitally necessary to you because they offer you an opportunity that is as essential to you as your original opportunity to grow your business: the chance to get out at the high point and start a fast-growth business all over again.

PART II

The Three Fast-Growth Leadership Strategies

2

Make Policy — Not Decisions

Your proper province as manager of a fast-profit-accumulating business is to make its growth policy. This is not the same as saying that you make the decisions; quite the contrary. If you are going to get a firm grip on the handles of your business so you can steer it to unusual growth, you must make sure that two things happen: You set policy and others below you make decisions about how to implement your policy.

If you misconceive your role to be an implementer, you will find it difficult to achieve fast growth. Policy is your blueprint for growth. As soon as you become an implementer, no one is left to make and enforce policy. Hire implementers; reward good ones well; but do not become one yourself.

What makes policy so central to your growth? Policy is the prime managerial act. It is the *allocation of always-scarce assets to seize the priority growth opportunities of the business*. If policy is wrong, your allocation of assets will be wrong. They will go to the wrong priorities or to nonpriorities. Opportunity will be missed or mismanaged. The business will fail to grow.

Getting your priorities right is the major role for you and for all growth managers. Policy makes sure that you fulfill it.

When you manage a growth business, policy is your first priority. You must make it your number one job. It cannot be

delegated. Instead, delegate operating decisions on how to execute policy in the most cost-effective manner. This is strategy
making, the province of middle management. Do not confuse it
with policy making. Strategies implement policy. Therefore,
you must never try to delegate policy making downward. If you
do, you will be delegating the growth leadership of your business along with it.

Make Policy by Managing ROI

Your standard of performance as policy-maker-in-chief is
the selection of growth objectives that cannot be achieved more
cost-effectively. To say the same thing in ROI terms, you are
making proper policy when your rate of return cannot be improved without adding to or subtracting from your investment
base. This says that you are allocating your assets optimally.

Policy making is the art of managing the ROI formula,
where return is the result when profit is divided by the investment required to achieve it. Policy should therefore dictate
minimizing the investment base of the business, running lean,
commensurate with maximizing the profit which is funded by
the investment. The word "commensurate" keeps profit and
investment in relationship. If investment is excessive in relation to the profit it produces, return suffers. If investment is too
lean, opportunity may go unrealized and return will again suf-
fer but perhaps at a later date.

In a fast-growth business, your eye should be on growing
profits. The investment denominator of the ROI formula
should be adjusted only in relation to maximizing profits from
sales. Growth management is a sales-driven discipline.

You, as a fast-growth manager, must represent maximum
profit objectives. You must be the Mr. Return of your business.
Every allocation you make must speak for your role. A wise
guideline to follow is this: Allocation without maximum return
is mismanagement.

If you are going to be Mr. Return, what is the role of your
middle managers? Each one of them is a Mr. or Ms. Investment, manager of the investment you have allocated to his or

her function. They are your collective decision makers, deciding how to invest after you have determined where and how much.

The standard of performance for your middle managers can best be related to your own in this way: They are making proper investment decisions when their objectives cannot be achieved with fewer dollars and need not be funded with more dollars. This means that their strategy decisions, each one of which represents an investment, are optimal.

Define Middle Managers as Strategic Investors

Because you are Mr. Return, you must seek to maximize growth profit. Because each of your middle managers is a Mr. Investment, together they seek to optimize their strategies that are designed to produce your growth profit objective. Is there a paradox here? Can the sum total of optimal strategies add up to a maximal return? Yes, because that is what maximal return is. If growth is to be calculated in real-world terms, it cannot be predicated on the rare possibility that you will be blessed with maximal strategies. Only optimal strategies can be hoped for. The return they produce will be the maximum that you can manage to call forth from your total resources, both your manpower capabilities and the investments they make.

Few managers understand the difference between policy and decisions, between asset allocation by objectives and strategic planning. As a result, growth falters. Instead of formulating and controlling policy, which is a full-time job, top managers allow themselves to become bogged down in strategy making. Some are beguiled by its creative challenge. Others lack good strategic planners. They sense the gap and try to fill it. Perhaps that is the game they themselves know best. If so, they will never leave it. This is why planners are rarely good growth managers. In other cases, strategy makers push upward to intrude on the policy process. If their early foothold is not chopped off, the neat division of labor between top and middle management will be blurred. So will results.

One president summed up his understanding of the policy-strategy distinction this way: "What do I work at every day that has to do with policy? About 20 percent of my time I spend making and revising it. That's the easy part of my job. The other 80 percent of the time I spend keeping my people from making decisions that can alter it. They try every way they can to make policy through strategy. I have to try twice as hard to be sure they make strategy that fits my policy." That, in brief, is running the business.

Reveal Policy Through Doctrines

Policy is your personal domain. It documents how you want to run your business to make it a fast grower of profits. You reveal policy through doctrines, the directives you publish that guide your middle managers in making their strategy decisions. Doctrine rules out strategy options you believe to be conducive to slow growth or no growth. It sets up channels for decision making that are designed to steer the implementation of your policy toward the fastest growth.

It is good management practice to keep the number of policies small. The prevalence of policies suggests that management does not know its business or how to grow it. Indeed, policies proliferate with unskilled or unknowledgeable managers. If you intend to manage smartly, you will probably not need more than three doctrines: a basic business positioning statement to force agreement on the nature of your market mission, an organization doctrine, and an operations doctrine.

BUSINESS POSITIONING DOCTRINE

How is your business to be positioned to each of its core markets so that it has the best chance to grow contribution from every one of them? In other words, how will you brand its value at a premium level?

Deciding the branding dilemma is only half the battle. The second half, and often the more difficult of the two, is to enshrine the positioning you arrive at into a doctrine so that everyone in your organization can adhere to it. Working with and through others, especially your own people, may be the essence of classical management, but it is always much more arduous and less controllable than working alone.

A positioning doctrine serves to keep your people from tampering with the market stance for your business that the doctrine sets forth. It compels adherence. All functions must conform to it so that everyone and everything that acts on your users relates to the basic positioning platform. Product benefits must correlate with your positioning. So must product packaging, sales promotion, and price. So must your sales and advertising approaches. So must the operating policies of the business.

What does a positioning doctrine need to say? It should spell out three things:

1. The market or markets in whose perception your premium business value is to be positioned.
2. The nature of the premium value to be perceived by your markets and its ratio to the premium price to be charged for it.
3. The margin of difference you are committed to maintain above the value positioning of major competitors.

No business, regardless of size or age, should attempt fast growth without a positioning doctrine. A small, relatively recent entrepreneurial business, Christine Valmy Inc., positions itself to be perceived by teenaged women and their mothers as the optimal source of advisory services and products to improve skin health and beauty. Exhibit 2 shows a positioning doctrine for a hugely larger and far longer established business, the American Telephone & Telegraph Company. The doctrine sets down a stance the company wants to preempt in its principal markets.

ORGANIZATION DOCTRINE

Either the form your organization takes will be conducive to growing fast or it will be a constraint. If you want it to be growth-conducive, you will have to gear it to represent your

Exhibit 2. AT&T Business Positioning Doctrine.

The business of the American Telephone & Telegraph Company is to be perceived by the heavy-profit-contributor segments of its commercial and industrial markets as offering premium values based on the combination of two benefits:

1. Optimal profit improvement delivered by the performance values of telecommunications systems, and
2. Maximum partnership values delivered by access to skilled, experienced business people and technical resources.

The market in whose perceptions these values are to be produced is composed of enterprises to which rapid, accurate internal and external information flow is vital to their cash flow and whose major business problems and opportunities are susceptible to cost-effective impact by telecommunications systems.

---

major markets rather than your products or process capabilities. In other words, you will have to *market-center* it around your key customer segments.

What businesses organize this way? IBM's data processing organization is divisionalized according to key markets, such as institutions and retail establishments. AT&T markets to business segment targets or districts. There are three of them: industrial, commercial, and a combination of government, education, and medicine. Xerox sells copiers by industry. Mead serves the homebuilding, education, and leisure markets by dedicated divisional clusters. General Electric and General Foods have strategic business units to serve major markets. NCR is organized according to major customer vocations. One of Monsanto's market centers, the Fire Safety Center, consolidates fire safety products from several sectors of the company and groups them separately according to building and construction, transportation, apparel, and furnishings markets. High technology companies are organized into customer provinces. Banks are administered in clusters of financial need groups.

A doctrine to legislate a market-centered form of organization should contain five component parts.

1. Each market center must be chartered to serve a major market composed of heavy profit contributors. Each market will have to be defined according to its primary needs. This will permit you to serve it by selling systems of your products and services that, taken together, can supply a combination of closely related benefits.

2. Each market center must be operated as a profit center. It must therefore be administered by an entrepreneurial business manager, the market center's chief line officer.

3. All operating functions of the parent business will act as supply services to support each market center's business manager.

4. The key asset of each market center will be its market information base, an up-to-date, accurate storehouse of the needs and buying preferences of the market it serves.

5. You and your staff must act as a central bank for your market-center managers. The central bank is a council of portfolio managers who, in holding-company fashion, counsel and fund the market-center business managers.

What does a market center look like? The basic organization structure is shown in Exhibit 3. Four service functions revolve around each business manager.

Development services combine market research and development with product R&D. *Control services* perform the basic research to evaluate the effectiveness of your established product and service marketing. They also provide the necessary recruitment, compensation and motivation, manpower training and development, legal, and financial functions. *Production services* coordinate engineering and manufacturing operations. *Promotion services* combine sales, advertising, and publicity.

What happens to parent-company marketing and its vice presidential function? There is no need for it. The entire organization is market-oriented. Each business manager acts as his own chief marketing officer.

Exhibit 3. Market-centered organization structure.

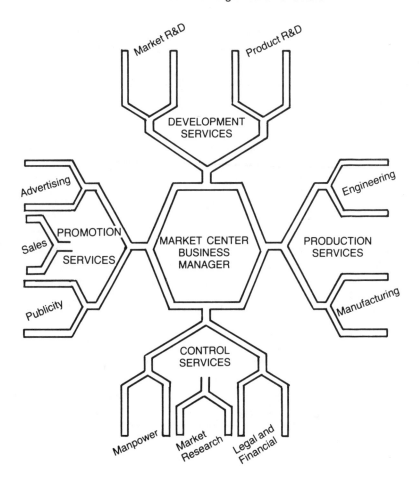

OPERATIONS DOCTRINE

Each major business operation should have its own doctrine that will insure three commitments.

1. All the people in the operation understand that they must be contributors to profit by building added units of value into

their operation; in other words, everyone must improve productivity.

2. Everyone understands that the ultimate standard of performance is that the products or services of the business can be marketed at a premium price.

3. Everyone understands that the ultimate judge of performance is the market served by the business and that market needs, preferences, and predispositions to buy must govern all operational decisions whether or not they directly relate to customers.

Give Teeth to Policy by Banking Money-Making Functions

All allocators of assets come to realize very quickly that the word *assets* is always preceded by a modifier, sometimes stated, sometimes implied. The modifier is *scarce* or *limited.* Assets are by their very nature insufficient. That is a fundamental characteristic of management. Demand for assets will exceed supply no matter how small or how large the supply. Mom-and-pop grocery stores complain about undercapitalization. So do General Motors and AT&T. All of them are correct.

Management is an exercise in chasing after objectives with insufficient assets. There is an unwritten law that institutionalizes this perverse relationship. Assets will always be fewer than the uses that can be planned for them. How can you solve this problem? One way is to obtain more assets. This is sometimes chancy, almost invariably expensive, and often self-defeating. No sooner are additional assets achieved than additional uses are planned for them. The other way to solve the problem of asset insufficiency is to allocate existing assets more stringently.

Scientific Data Systems is an example of a fast-growing business that deliberately courted the hazards of undercapitalization and has merchandised them well. SDS started as a bootstrap venture with a shoestring budget of only $500,000. "I believe in management being lean and hungry, in having to strain and push to be successful," its president has said. "It's psychologically healthy to start skinny."

When it began business, the company's offices and manufacturing plant were crammed into 2,000 square feet of space in a leased corner of a Los Angeles factory. There were only ten employees. The individual work load was heavy. Productivity was extremely high.

The president and his four managers regularly put in more than 60 hours a week. At the outset, they formed a skeletal team consisting of a vice president of software development and directors of engineering, manufacturing, and marketing. Each man performed many duties. When additional positions were ready to be filled for controller and directors of field service, material control, and marketing support, equity was used to reserve managers who could not yet be put on the payroll. Candidates were offered stock holdings for as little as $10,000 and the promise of a salaried job three years later.

A direct field sales force was beyond budget. So SDS sold only to distributors and original equipment manufacturers. Nonetheless, the company knew its priorities. It invested significant sums in training its distributors in customer service.

Growing a business requires you to be a tough-minded banker; that is, an unrelenting partisan as an allocator. What are our money-making functions? What are our big-winner products? Where are our heaviest profit-contributing markets? Invest in them and starve the rest.

All growth, and faster-than-average growth in particular, comes about as the result of disproportionate investment. Growing a business and running a balanced business are two different management styles. In one instance, every petitioner for money receives a fair share. Even when all budgets are knocked down to zero every year and then built back up, tradition and the highly subjective concept of fairness come into play to defeat, or at least adulterate, reasoned parsimony. In the case of growth management—management by deliberate unbalance—the big-needer markets and the big-winner products get the lion's share of funds. All else gets by.

In spite of the fact that all businesses are different, can useful generalizations be made about money-making functions that will typically reward forced feeding with a high-return contribution to growth? Entrepreneurial managers seem to concentrate on two such functions. One is plowing up market facts. The second is plowing market facts back into their product's development, production, and marketing.

PLOW DEEP: DIG UP MARKET FACTS

No matter how a market — a group of people who share common needs — is defined, markets are essentially where the money is. Since markets are the bedrock funders of your growth, it makes sense to begin your growth thrust by going first to them to assay how much they will pay to do business with you.

How much a market will pay is the critical dimension of market research, not what it will buy or why. There is a subtle fact that makes this so. Markets will buy more products and services than they will pay a premium price for. Yet premium price is your fountainhead of growth.

You cannot grow a business fast, or grow it at all, without being knowledgeable about your market's needs to solve its problems and take advantage of its opportunities, what its preferences are for solutions that will benefit its needs, and why it will buy its solutions from one source of supply rather than others. For any growth-dedicated business these are the essential elements of information, or EEI as they are called by military campaigners. But it is possible to know these elements, essential as they are, and still fail to grow unless the most essential element of all is known: Will your market pay you a premium price for your solution, and how high can the price be?

Market research is successful or unsuccessful on the basis of whether it leads to growth profits through its ability to interpret customer preferences for premium price. All research brings back information, so general learning per se cannot be a valid research objective. Even specific learning may not be valid unless it contains what, for growth purposes, is *the* market fact: the upper-limit boundary of a market's price sensitivity. This is the crucial clue to your value-to-price ratio since your growth will come from the delivery of a premium value that exceeds the market's maximum price.

Plowing a market's value perceptions and unearthing its

sense of the worth of your ability to add most to those values is the single most critical developmental strategy for your fast growth. It develops your eventual growth positioning in your marketplace. Accordingly, it should be your first investment. Nothing can precede it because all else is sequentially dependent on its findings. It should also be a recurring investment. Values change, and when they do, value-to-price ratios can change inside market minds as a response. To be caught unaware of such a change is to subject your growth objective to the highest risk.

Marketplaces are value battlegrounds. Never forget that you are the sole spokesman for the preservation of your market's value perception in your favor. Every other factor in the marketplaces you serve is a contrary force. A competitor is a value destabilizer. He seeks to alter the market's perception of your value-to-price ratio by diminishing the premium nature of your value and emphasizing the premium nature of your price. If you can be made to appear to be overpriced, he wins. New technologies may further destabilize your value, as do legislative changes that constrain you, changes in your own organization that diminish or add to your capability to deliver value, and changes in your market's values that come about as a result of social and economic dynamics.

The only defenses you have against this perpetual onslaught of changes are market research to provide you with early warning and marketing, your sole witness, to state your case. Both must therefore be unexcelled.

How much should you invest to study your market's propensity to pay you a premium price? Your budget, whatever it turns out to be, will be a percentage of sales. But it should not be calculated that way. Deriving a research investment based on previous sales makes research a result of sales. Instead, it should be exactly the opposite. Research should be a cause of sales; more specifically, it should be a cause of premium-priced sales.

Your research of market needs and preferences should be budgeted on a task basis. There are two questions to be asked. How much is required to take a statistically projectable sample of your market and get into its perceptions of problems and opportunities, the benefits it prefers to obtain in order to meet its needs, and the maximum boundaries of its price acceptance? The answer to this question will determine the intensity of the research (how deep you must probe) and how extensive it must be (how large a sample you must probe into). The second question is, how often must you go back to the market and revalidate your findings? The answer to this question will determine the frequency of the research.

A few ground rules may help. Dynamic markets such as consumer packaged foods, drugs, and cosmetics may require quarterly or at least semiannual probes. So may markets that are in competitive turmoil or technological flux. More stable markets may be probed annually. No market should remain unstudied longer than 12 months unless you plan to abandon it —which, in effect, you will be doing if you leave it to your assumptions about its needs for such a long period of time.

Fund liberally, interpret stringently is a wise motto for market research. This may mean a budget that has a 1 to 1.5 percent relation to annual sales in a $20 million business. Or it may mean a budget with a minimum 0.5 percent relation to sales in a company with yearly revenues of $200 million. The key criterion, though, is not the percentage. It is the adequacy of the investment to teach you how to locate a market's premium price spot.

You will find it difficult to overspend on market research. But if you follow your industry average, you will almost surely underspend. Average expenditures foster average growth. To grow fast means that you will outrun average accumulations of market fact. Superior growth requires superior knowledge.

PLOW BACK: FERTILIZE PRODUCT AND MARKETING

What do you do with your market fact base? How do you pay off the investment? Since the objective of research is to help you maintain premium price, you must plow back into product development the research findings about your market's needs for value. By doing so, you can transform your products into delivery systems for market values. You must also plow back your research findings into marketing so that your sales, advertising, and publicity can be delivery systems for the same market values.

Your products and their marketing carry an enormous burden. They are the only external missionaries of your commitment to provide premium values as your tradeoff for superior growth. They are your only outputs that your markets ever see. Your plans, your capabilities, your internal investments, your processes, and most of your nonselling people remain obscure to your users. Whether you succeed or fail is based on the value of your twin delivery systems, your products and their marketing. Both of them need to be fertilized with market facts. They also need to be fertilized with major investments.

Instilling market values into the product – as opposed to filling it with technical construction or performance values – must precede instilling market values into your marketing. Ethics aside, to market value that is absent in the product is to become your own competitor. Markets cannot get values out if you do not put them in. If they try and fail, they will charge you for the effort and add a surcharge for breach of promise. They will devalue you. Whatever your original ratio of price to value, you will thenceforth appear to be overpriced. The market will dry up as a source of your growth funds.

Equally devastating, and equally inexcusable, is failure to fertilize your marketing with the facts of market value. Your markets will buy your product only if they buy its marketing first; that is, if they perceive its superior value-to-price ratio. Far greater numbers of heavy profit-contributing users, both actual and potential, will be served by your marketing than by your product. Furthermore, most of them will receive the value it contains in advance of their use of the product. Your marketing will act as the product's advance man; *promotion precedes product.* Unless your marketing makes buying the product appear to be necessary in order to obtain its premium value, it will not be doing its job. It is the value added by marketing that will in reality predetermine your product's purchase.

Marketing should be the fatted cow of your growth investment fund. You should invest to make sure that you are positioning the product properly. Are you correlating its most critical benefit values with the market's most critical needs? Are you valuing your benefit at a premium so that value will exceed even a premium price?

You should invest to make sure that you are selling, advertising, and publicizing your premium value with sufficient impact. What is impact? Three factors, apart from the proper delivery of the value, determine it: the continuity of your marketing campaign (how long it continues to go to market); its frequency (how often); and its media mix (how it combines the three delivery systems of sales, advertising, and publicity for maximum cost-effectiveness).

Your sales function and your advertising will almost invariably be your major delivery systems for the value added by marketing as well as for the product itself. The sales function should be regarded principally as an agent for adding marketing value and only secondarily as an agent for delivering physical products. Otherwise, your sales force will not truly sell. It will not add a perceived premium value in advance of the product. It will just deliver. You will have a product-driven sales force as a consequence and, along with it, low commodity margins and slow growth or no growth.

What about advertising? In this context, how should you use it? Advertising has the same basic mission as sales: to demonstrate a premium value that enables your premium price to be accepted as fair. In most businesses, no other marketing strategy can deliver this perception of added value so frequently and with such perfect control of the style and content of the message.

Fund Your Key People Who Execute Policy

After market knowledge, your key people are your greatest resource. Without market information they will be helpless. They will not be able to grow your business except by chance. Market research is an investment in improving their chance.

Who are the key people essential to your fast growth—or, in other words, who are your principal internal customers for

market research information? These will be your growth lieu-
tenants, the strategy decision makers who run the functions
that are the most vital for your growth.

If you believe that the 80-20 rule applies to powering your
principal functions, this suggests that relatively few processes
in your business control a disproportionately large share of
your growth potential. This is generally true. There are most
likely to be power principals. In most businesses, there are
three of them: the principal who controls your sales, the principal who controls your product research and engineering, and
the principal who controls your finances. In terms of relative
importance, they are an equal trinity.

Your sales and product engineering functions determine
what you sell and how much of it you can move at a premium
price. These are two sides of the same coin. In a growth organization, each of these functional managers should be top-rated.
There is no substitute for superior capability in either position.
Each manager must know more than the management of one
function. Each must also know how to integrate the management of both functions.

Sales and product engineering; product engineering and
sales. They must be partners. In order to sell in volume at a
premium price, the product must have premium values engineered into it. How will they get there? Among other ways,
your sales manager should be the resident ambassador of market values to product engineering. How will the engineered
values be translated into marketable values? Among other
ways, your product engineering manager should be their official translator to sales. It is imperative that they speak to each
other. Even more important, they must be able to talk in the
common language of the market: not in technical jargon, not in
sales-speak but in words that express the values of customers
that determine premium price.

If you can imagine a product engineering director and a
director of sales speaking a common language rooted in premium price, you will have no trouble including your chief financial officer in the mix. His language should already be the
common denominator of growth management because growth
is profit growth, and profit growth depends on premium price.

Your financial manager must be sensitive to users — not bankers or shareholders — as the source of your growth funds. Their qualitative values, which determine their propensity to pay a premium price, must be respected along with the quantitative contribution they can make to profits.

All three of your key managers must agree on who originates the growth of your business: your markets. They must agree on the definition of business purpose for your organization: to be the best benefiter of market needs by providing the best premium value. They must agree on their joint overriding purpose: to command premium price. In short, they must be the team that *brands* your business and the products or services you market.

Use Independent Counsel as Supplementary Policy Executors

Manpower is a make-or-buy decision. Sales, product engineering, and finance must be made in house. Two other kinds of principal people can be brought in from the outside as consultants on a periodic or continuing basis. They can provide you and your staff with cost-effective counsel that you may not need to retain as ongoing resources and that, in any case, you would not be able to attract or retain as employees. One is supplementary technical counsel. The second is counsel in growth management planning.

The contribution that can be made by consultants in your existing technology or in technologies that represent logical extensions from it is twofold. They can add new knowledge, increasing the capability of your R&D and product engineering staffs. They can also help implement the commercialization of new or current knowledge so that your product engineering function can be more cost-effective.

What about growth management planning counsel? It can keep you from the pitfalls and pratfalls of managing your growth in a cost-ineffective manner. By preserving you against error, growth counsel can help you reduce the time costs and dollar costs of fast growth. Think of the benefits as time compression and cost saving. There is also another benefit. Good growth counsel can help insure your profit-making timetable. If it can assist you in achieving your growth objectives on time, it will be more than worth its professional fee. If it can help you achieve your objectives one month, one week, or even one day early, your return on the investment you make in it can ever so much further exceed its cost.

When you engage growth counsel in this way, you assign it the role of guarantor of your objectives. The consultant does not act as a surrogate manager who will preempt your leadership. You acquire a limited partner, not a rival. Your hand remains the only hand to touch the wheel. The consultant's hand touches only your own. Consultants can serve you in three ways.

1. They can help you rationalize your growth objectives, putting intellectual pressure on you to enlarge them or shrink the time frame for their achievement if they appear to be too conservative or, contrariwise, to diminish them or stretch their time frame if they appear too venturesome.

2. They can help you search out optional growth strategy mixes to achieve your objectives, advocate alternate strategies, and recommend various mixes of investment and timing so as to increase the odds of your fielding the most cost-effective campaign.

3. They can help you monitor the rate and volume of profit growth in comparison to your plan, help you anticipate and correct deviations, and act as a barking watchdog when events appear to be conspiring to throw you seriously off plan.

Insist that your growth consultants return more than your investment in their services. This will enable them to be bargains. Reward them on the basis of the value they return, not on the time it takes them to do it. This will enable them to be premium-price bargains—the same as your own products and services.

3
Manage People — Not Functions

Businesses are more people-determined than function-determined. Success in growing fast depends on people. This must be so since all businesses have virtually the same functions; the departments and processes of one business are nearly identical to all others in the same industry. Yet not all businesses are similarly successful. What makes the difference? The premium is on people — the people who manage the business functions.

Growth is hastened when management style favors people, not functions. Growth managers manage their managers. They manage the manager of their sales function, for example, not the function itself. And so with their other function managers.

What does it mean to manage people: not to manage *through* people or *with* people but to manage people? It means three things. One is that you must manage directively, according to policy, instead of participatively. The second is that you must manage by standards of performance instead of by motivation. The third is that you must manage on the basis of shared rewards instead of on salary-based compensation arrangements.

Manage According to Policy

The purpose of policy is to rule out management by partici-pation. Policy, by its very nature, is arbitrary. It is not just the top manager's prerogative. It is also his prescription for fast growth. Since you have the albatross of profit responsibility, you must also have the privilege of setting forth the policy commandments by which growth profits can be made. The al-batross cannot be shared. Policy making cannot be shared either.

Managing according to policy deters the adulterative effects of managing by participation. The act of allocating assets permits a growth manager to direct his organization's in-vestments according to *where* they must go. *How* they are implemented is second-level management's ballgame. By rec-ommending *how*, middle managers participate in fast growth. But they must stay out of the *where*.

Why is directive management superior to broad-scale par-ticipative management—in which middle managers have their say in policy formation—when a business wants to grow fast?

In the evolutionary history of participative management, group influence in business organizations originated in com-modity companies. Slow growth or no growth predominated. Managers were bored; the business was going nowhere. As a result, they could not see where it might end up and most of them simply did not understand their role in helping it get there. Frustrated and reduced to mechanistic, repetitive deci-sion making, they wanted more. Since they could not agitate for more money in a profit-pressed business, they asked for more participation in setting its objectives and standards.

Participative management could not have arisen in an en-trepreneurial growth business because everyone is moving ahead with the business too fast to be bored, frustrated, or isolated from its achievements and the checkpoints that pro-claim its progress.

CREATE POLICY FIRST—THEN RALLY THE TEAM

There is a tried and true injunction about how to succeed beyond the norm in organizing a business: "Find the man," the growth leader. The injunction should be supplemented by the words, "and the team." No man or woman can grow a significant business alone. But *the man* is still central. He must define the business. He must charter its objectives. He must allocate its assets. And he must select his team. Perhaps it is equally true to say that his team must also select him. The single most important determinant in assembling a team is the compatibility its members feel with your policy. This is not a chicken or egg situation. Which must come first is obvious. Policy must take precedence over team selection. This is the only way a team can know beforehand the financial, organizational, and operating base of the business to which you will ask them to pledge allegiance.

Policy differences are the bane of management unity. What they mean is that someone wants an asset to be allocated in a different manner. No business that has fast growth as its fundamental philosophy can afford policy splits. Yet they will be inevitable if you permit policy to be a subject of participative decision making instead of directing it yourself and leaving your second-level team to decide on the implementation of your policy.

The ideal way to found a growth business is to hack out its policy first, then — and only then — call for others to come forward and rally around it. Constitutional conventions, congresses, caucuses, and committees are poor devices for creating policy. No doubt they will generate *policies* — diverse, disharmonious, and mutually diluting — in conference rooms that call to mind aviaries of chattering magpies. But pluralistic policies require a great compromiser to make them even appear unified, let alone actually be unified. No growth business can originate in compromise. It must have one policy maker and one body of policy. Every key manager on its growth team must subscribe to policy as a good soldier and an all-year-round patriot. You must be their general.

DARE TO BE SUBJECTIVE—EVEN ARBITRARY

The concentration of policy making in one leader and the personal and subjective, even arbitrary, nature of its content are among the most distinguishing characteristics of growth business. They are little known and less practiced in traditional corporate organizations. There, concern is expressed at a heightened level for the U/A factor: the understanding of all participants in the purpose of each project and their acceptance of its mission as well as their own roles in it. The U/A factor is especially prevalent in matrix organizations where commercial and technical resources are separately structured and must find a unifying corporate sponsor to bring them together into a team. Matrix teams are generally devoid of entrepreneurial leadership. It is no mere coincidence that fast-growth entrepreneurial businesses are not organized along matrix lines. They are the organizational kiss of death to growth.

When IBM was young and in its entrepreneurial phase of development, Tom Watson stood before his people and laid down policy. Assets would thenceforth flow chiefly to marketing. Customer knowledge would be the company's most important resource, the base from which all products and promotion would flow. The sales force would sell as consultants to their customers. Key-account customers would be converted to loyal, long-term clients. The consultative sales force objective would be to improve customer profit, not sell computer systems. For this, IBM would command a premium price. Premium profits would follow. The entire organization would live as it sold – by being the most cost-effective processor of information about its markets and then marketing the output in the twin forms of the product and selling style.

Cooperation, compliance, and commitment were invited. So were résumés from any IBM people who preferred to vend computers to hardware-oriented, price-sensitive customers at low margins under intense competition. A generation or so later, Jack Vollbrecht and Bob Katkov stood before their people at Aerojet-General and gave them a similar charge. Of course, you are good at your functions, they said to their conglomerate company's functional specialists. When you work within our growth policy, you will find yourselves even more fully liberated. You will be able to get an even higher yield from your talents. This will be to your benefit as well as to ours.

Without gainsaying the importance of understanding and

acceptance – after all, how can men and women work together without them? – we must recognize that the principal factor in growth management is the W factor: *where* the money goes, *where* the concentration is, and *where* the objectives are set. To the extent that the W factor originates in the mind of the growth manager and is popularized by him, standardized by him, and symbolized by him, to that extent will fast growth be assured.

Manage by Standards of Performance

How do you motivate your team to produce for you? Does the stick work best, or the carrot . . . or some rhythmic combination of the two? You can tell no one knows for sure because there are so many remedies on the market, each put forth by its own school of small group dynamicists, hierarchical behaviorists, or transactional analysts. But, as in any field, many remedies bespeak the fact that there is no cure.

Fast growth in a business environment is invariably accomplished by small bands of self-motivated people. They require little or no motivation from outside sources. In fact, they need to be left alone more than to be massaged, tickled, or prodded. Other people's objectives have faint appeal to them. Galvanized by a leader whose self-interest matches their own and whose neck, like theirs, is on the line, they can move the commercial equivalent of mountains.

All of us need motive power to make us go. Fast-growth managers and their teams are no exceptions. What moves them? The thrusts that propel people to enter high-reward situations at higher-than-average risk are not reflected in the propagandistic adjectives that corporations like to apply to their people in their annual reports or to talk about when they go recruiting. Instead, they are made up of personal characteristics that are usually ignored or referred to only euphemistically. What are they?

LOOK FOR SELFHOOD—AND ITS EXPRESSIONS

Fast-growth managers and teams have a high component of self in their personal inventories. In addition to being self-motivated, they are self-actuating, self-centered, and *self*ish.

They are high achievers. Their governing need is to excel: to exceed norms, to win out in competition, to win over rivals, to come in first. For many of them, there is no such thing as second place. There is first place and all others. All others are last.

Fixation on winning tends to make workaholics out of entrepreneurial business growers. Work is their occupation and preoccupation. Not only does it occupy them, their time, and their energies; they occupy it, filling it up with their commitment.

Sometimes this causes them to appear narrow. Anything unrelated to their area for achievement is extraneous. Few companies boast of the narrowness of their managers. Instead, they invest small fortunes in training them to be well-rounded when it is the narrow, pointed ones who could lead them to new growth.

Growth managers are frequently accused of being materialists. The good ones are. They want an incremented bottom line so badly they can taste it. Most high achievers would work as hard to grow as fast even if they were not paid for it. But money and the things it will buy are their maximum symbols of success. They do not simply love money; they lust for it. It is their topmost reward. At any given moment somewhere in the world, an industrial psychologist is telling some corporation's top management that their managers value money rewards far less than recognition, acclaim, executive perquisites, affiliation, or anything else. At that precise moment, a growth manager laughs to himself and then goes back to making money.

So what have we here in people who meet the stereotype of fast growers of businesses? They are self-centered and work-centered to the point where self and work blend into one. Work is the sweetest expression of their inner selves. In turn, their inner selves are nowhere so well expressed as at work. Narrow and pointed, they have a sharpness that often sticks others. They are materialistic, lustful after money and its rewards. Hyper people, always turned on, they are remarkably resistant to the encouragements or discouragements of others.

This is a unique profile, to say the least. In your mind's ear, can you hear a corporate president extolling the traits of his corporateurs in this way? Shareholders might be offended. But securities analysts might be delighted.

If growth managers do not require traditional motivational inducements, or if they may react negatively instead of positively to them, how can their energies be made productive? The answer is not more and better motivators; it is standards of performance.

SET STANDARDS THAT MOTIVATE—NOT JUST MEASURE

In an entrepreneurial organization, performance standards are not just substitutes for motivation. They *are* motivation. They set the norms which are to be exceeded. They give the fast-growth team something to shoot at. Meet the standards and you are in the fast-growth ballpark. Go beyond them to set new standards that have never before been achieved and you will be in the Hall of Fame. What do you do for an encore? You do it again, this time better than before. How often do you do it? You are always doing it since it is your life cycle as well as your work cycle. When do you stop? When you retire. When do you retire? When you are taken by the kindly hand of death.

Fast-growth managers maximize the return they get on the allocation of their assets by setting standards of high performance for their prime mover teams of business growers. The standard of performance for all the implementing functions — especially sales and product engineering — must be superior to the standards enjoyed by slow-growth or no-growth commodity business managers. Performance may be deemed to be met when standards are fulfilled — in other words, when growth management is *adequate.* Performance standards must therefore be understood to be minimal standards. The intent must clearly be that they will be exceeded — in other words, that growth management will be *superior.*

Manage on the Basis of Shared Rewards

What do you really risk when you opt for fast growth? The answer may be unexpected. No, it is not security. If you are a legitimate fast-growth manager, you will feel secure only when you are growing a business fast. Nor is it your career safety or even solvency that is at risk. The real risk that all fast-growth managers take is in being successful yet not being invited to share in the success to which they have contributed. Apply this to your team. For them, nothing defeats the achievement of growth more than not sharing in it. The converse is equally true. Nothing incites the fullest measure of their devotion to growth more than a share in its rewards.

Salary-based compensation schemes simply do not incite devotion. Performance bonuses that may double a man's salary come close. But receiving more money and sharing in the enterprise are not the same. Sharing means one of two things, sometimes both. An equity share in the business, whether in real or phantom stock, imbeds a manager in the fate of his business as a co-owner. Instead of working for someone else or for someone else's business, he is growing his own value. A second method of sharing is with a royalty on sales. This makes every member of the growth team market-sensitive, with a raised consciousness directed to meeting customer perceptions of premium value that fast growth depends on.

If you are a growth manager, you should insist on a share in the rewards of your business. You should also grant sharing to your prime mover growth team members.

As a narrow band of men, you can then take on the all-for-one, one-for-all attitude of colleagues. Many collegial groups of business growers display a hint of paranoia about the real world around them. They see, or profess to see, that the world is a conspiracy against their growth. Costs continually rise, forcing up breakeven and delaying or diminishing the onset of profit. Competitive pressure forces down price, further shrinking profit. Technological innovation compresses the growth phase of the life cycle curve within which premium profits can be earned. These forces, along with legislated costs that make no contribution to productivity, inflationary erosion of the value of profits, and variations in market demand, always appear to conspire against growth objectives. Sharing the suspicion that this is so can be a strong bond between you and your growth colleagues, as potent a driving force as owning shareholds or deriving royalties.

It is difficult to describe this suspicion which most growth organizations come to have. One way may be to call it a beleaguered feeling: the sense of being at risk, surrounded by inimical and even hostile forces yet determined to hold on and triumph. Some growth managers have described it as a feeling akin to patriotism. Others have given it a religious cast, emphasizing its dedication to the belief that fast growth is the true nature of their business and that they will overcome no matter what the odds. If you prefer the religious theme, be careful on two counts. Do not act like a martyr. And be sure to bring your growth profits in the door during this life, not the one beyond.

Think of Yourself as Running a Novel Cat Skinnery

Growth is a breakthrough business. Previous profit bogeys must be broken through. So must handed-down attitudinal boundaries that are traditional within commodity companies: keep a low profile, don't volunteer, don't stick your neck out, and always protect your derriere. Businesses are grown by neck-sticker-outers. In commodity organizations, you may see a sign that says, "Regard the turtle. He never gets anywhere until he sticks his neck out." You never see this sign in a growth business. All necks are out to begin with.

There are other ingrained attitudes that will also have to go by the board. They concern reasons for employing or rejecting certain strategies. The fact that competition is doing it or is not doing it is not a reason. The fact that it has been tried before and failed or that it has never been tried before is no reason either. The hunch that there must be something wrong with it because it seems so simple is no reason to walk away from it. Most strokes of genius are simple, which is why they work. The fear that something will not be productive because it is new and unproven deserves careful consideration. After all, the argument goes, if it had been any good someone else would have thought of it first or done it long ago. But novelty, in and of itself, is no reason for scorn.

Some of the greatest growth thrusts have come about because someone did something innovative, often because he did not know it was novel and many times by chance. Royal Crown created a once-in-a-lifetime growth explosion with Diet Rite Cola principally by stocking it in the regular soft drink section of supermarkets instead of the diet section. (Can you still hear all the voices saying, "It will never sell there"?) Ford had a once-in-a-lifetime success with the Mustang by building the car almost from the ground up on the findings of market research, including a potential buyer profile so accurate that Ford dealers could spot Mustang prospects when they walked into the showroom. (Can you still hear all the voices saying, "Why should we ask people what they want in a car? Isn't it our job to know?")

Boeing commercialized the jet airplane and captured the market while McDonnell Douglas and Lockheed tried to get one more generation of sales out of piston engines. (Can you still hear all the voices saying, "They'll fall flat on their faces; the market is nowhere near ready for jets"?) IBM added significant growth profits to its mainframe computer business when it marketed an innovative series of machines at a time when its then-current models were still selling extremely well. (Can you still hear all the voices saying, "They'll never deliberately obsolete their present equipment; it'll still be what we will have to compete against next year"?) And in business after business, including your own, can you still hear all the voices saying "They'll never get the price down," or "they'll never get the volume" or "the distribution" or "a sales force hired and trained on time"?

If you want to play the fast-growth game, you have a choice of menu. You can order the traditional businessman's platter and eat crow with humble pie. Or you can dine on skinned cat if you skin it in novel ways. A growth business can be characterized as a novel cat skinnery. Within the circumscriptions of policy, every encouragement should be given to your middle managers to make their strategy decisions as novel as possible. "How many ways can you skin the same cat?" is the first challenge to give them in their strategy decision making. The second challenge: "Which way is the most cost-effective?"

Manage Yourself

The strategy of managing people rather than functions applies to your self-management as well as to the management of your prime mover team. You must manage yourself as the principal inside resource of the business. This makes you the correlate in importance to your market, which is the principal outside resource. You are "the man." Your personal management style and the content of your policy are the critical factors in the fast growth of your lbusiness.

MANAGE THE FIVE GOLDEN RULES

Many growth managers live by five golden rules of self-management.

Rule one is to *manage yourself as if you are an investment banker* to your business. Think of the business as representing your sole investment. Think of yourself as its major investor. This will help you see the business as it really is—a financial instrument whose purpose is to return growth profits. It will also help you see your own role in managing the business as you really must be—a financial backer whose purpose is to maximize your return.

If you take the position of principally having a fiduciary relationship with your business, you will have a singular advantage. You will be better able to resist the tender traps of becoming romantically involved with its products to the point where you may try to maximize their technical inputs or their market share instead of their contribution to profit.

The return-on-investment thinking that this mind set fosters will aid you in making and revising appropriations, setting and enforcing policy, and conducting yourself in proper growth business style. To be growth-minded, in this sense, means that you quite literally mind your business: that is, you become a bottom-liner who runs a tight shop that brings in the bucks.

By taking an investment banker approach, you will help yourself remember rule two, which enjoins you to *nail down your policy and at the same time always keep your strategy options open.* Policy must be nailed because it is the hallmark of leadership. It tells your prime mover team what kind of business you are running and where you plan to take it — and to take them along with it. Policy must be unequivocal. Objectives must be crystal clear. The principles that govern funding for the hot buttons must be assured. Otherwise, even if there is growth, it will be unprincipled.

To the same extent that policy must be nailed, the strategies by which your allocations are to be transformed into superior profits must be kept flexible. A more cost-effective strategy should always be substituted for one that is more costly or less effective. Innovative decision making should be encouraged at all times, not just while business plans are being prepared and before they are approved. Strategies, which are the ways your business is going to get to the profit objectives you have set for it, must be continually re-joined to changing situational values inside and outside the business. They must be free to move when need or opportunity presents itself.

No organization can survive, let alone grow, if its policies are subject to frequent change or are fuzzy or are communicated so vaguely that they appear to be altered from one expression to another. For this reason, you must be the single professor of policy: its one source and its final interpreter. This must be your stern visage. Alternatively, you must remain in an invitational mode to receive new strategy recommendations all the time. This is your open visage, opening you to the full richness of inputs from your staff without constraints that are either actual or implied.

A third rule is for you to *make yourself highly visible* to your people, to the key decision makers and influencers in your major markets, to your industry's trade association, and to the investment community. Fill them with awareness of your policy, first of all, and then with a close linkage of your policy to yourself as its driving force. This is not to suggest that you be preoccupied with self-promotion. Rather, it is the business that must be promoted; for best results, it should be propagandized by you.

Growth businesses are frequently known by their chief grower's personal image. *The* business becomes personalized as *your* business. This gives you a proprietary relationship with your organization and its people. It, as well as they, comes to bear your personal imprint. This does not make them your clones. What it does is to make them growth partners who can identify with you, their leader, as well as with your growth objectives.

If your own personal style has an identity with the style of your business, reflecting it and making it come alive as its most tangible symbol, you will feel the one-to-oneness of your role as it is played back to you from inside and outside sources alike. This, in turn, will further bond you to the business. Louis XIV identified himself one to one with the state. "I am the state," he said. You should instead say, "I am the business."

The fourth rule involves you and your people. In the same way that the business is the chief representative and projection of you, you must *gain your people's commitment* to a similar allegiance by acting as the chief representative of your business with them.

There are two ways to do this other than the extremely personal strategy of half fear, half respect employed by George Patton and Vince Lombardi. One way is to charge your staff to implement policy. This will require you to communicate policy. It will also cause you to politick inside your business to urge your team's adherence to it, assure yourself that they understand it, and monitor their compliance with it. Growth leaders are much like politicians who run for office by merchandising their platforms. They must be out in the limelight, getting what is known as good press for their electioneering.

The second way to gain commitment is by individual social contacts with your prime mover team. Each contact can serve to reinforce the pledges to preserve, protect, and defend policy in the course of their implementation. This approach engenders a high level of understanding for your policy and a familiarity with its terms. As your key people sign off on the same policy commitments again and again, they can establish something of the same one-to-one identification with the business that you have.

The fifth rule is for you to *be chief publicist of your growth achievements* as they occur, acting as corporate spokesman for reaching the profit objectives of the business. This symbolizes you as the harbinger of good news. It also reaffirms the dynamism of the organization, reassures everyone that fast growth is indeed attainable, and permits the intense bonding that occurs among people when success is shared.

The composite of these five golden rules will add up to your management style as a business grower. Most fast growers of businesses have similar profiles. The rules are a fraternal badge, making corporateurs more alike than different no matter what their industry. No-growers and slow-growers resemble each other, too, across industry lines. You can always tell which badge you are displaying by the people who are attracted to you. Likes attract. Opposites are the ones who will never understand you.

4

Be a Builder
of Customer Businesses —
Not Just a Seller to Them

What is the one best way to grow your business? There is a single answer. Grow the value of your customers' businesses. Help them make more profit as the result of doing business with you. Teach them to be profit-making investors in the rewards you offer. Then teach them how to reinvest their return in adding still greater values to their businesses through applying more of your products and services. Demonstrate the unique benefits of a planned partnership with you.

If you do these things, your customers will be unable to escape growth. Their growth will leave you no recourse but to grow in response.

Customers have already been described as sources of funds. Now we can amplify that definition. *Customers are the sources of growth funds.* They are the true sponsors of your profits. You are, in effect, in their employ as a grower of their businesses just as much as you are in the employ of your own business. Without them, you cannot speed your growth. Without you, they cannot speed theirs.

Perhaps this is what old-time entrepreneurs mean when they say, "Take care of your customers and they will take care of you." A good growth relationship with your key customers is essentially a mutual aid pact: You help me grow and I will help you grow. Your marketing plan plays the role of documenting this pact. Customer growth must be its tonic chord, the central theme that runs throughout its strategy mix.

Customer growth must also be the basic positioning of your business. Why are you in business? "We are in business to help our customers speed their growth." And you yourself, in your style, your policies, and your role as definer of your business, must speak out clearly for customer profit enhancement at every opportunity.

How does enshrining customer growth at the top of your hierarchy of management values square with the traditional concept of operating businesses to grow the values of the shareholders? There is no conflict. Increased shareholder values — your own included — are the end objective. Increased customer values are the means. If you achieve the means, the end result will follow.

Quick-Screen Your Business Growth Style

If growing customer businesses is your means to the fast growth of your own business, it should become the focal point of your entire organization and operating strategy. Your business must be built around it. Do you have a policy that countermands it? You must correct it. Do you have an organization structure that retards it? You must redesign it. Do you have operations that nullify it, delay its implementation, make it more costly or less effective? You must remodel your business — literally, remake the operating model on which you have been functioning.

To further your dedication, your market research will be out in the field, testing the upper limits of premium price acceptance in each of your markets and then bringing into your business the customer values that you must benefit in order to merit the premium. What about your other functions? The rest of your business can be looked on as being dedicated to bringing these customer values back to the customers.

This is an all-encompassing dedication. You cannot just adopt it at sales campaign time. It is not a gimmick. If it is going to be the operating code you live by, it will have to become your main yardstick. You have a potential new product opportunity. Will it help your customers grow? You are tempted to renovate an existing product line. Will it help your customers grow? You can open up new distribution channels, redeploy your sales force, relocate your warehouses, electronically control your manufacturing scheduling, retheme your advertising, revise your order entry system or inventory control, make a meger, or acquire a new technology. Will it help your customers grow?

If it will not, you will be hard-pressed to make it help your own business grow.

The next time you hear someone tell you his business is market-oriented or customer-sensitive or user-driven, ask him if he does these things. If he doesn't, he isn't. Few managers are. In the final analysis, this is why the great majority of businesses grow slowly or not at all. They do not help their customers grow fast enough. Their customers therefore do not help them grow fast enough either. Fair enough, isn't it?

When you turn the crank that sets your business going every morning, you already know how you can grow fast. You need the premium profits that accrue from premium prices. Are you as well advised on how your customers can grow fast? In other words, do you know why they will find it acceptable to pay you a premium price as their investments in rapid growth? There are only two reasons. They tell you what the purpose of your business must be and what final product it must deliver. You will have to reduce customer costs more than the price you charge to reduce them. Or you will have to increase customer revenues on the same basis.

With this in mind, you can conduct a quick-screen evaluation of your business-growing style. Are you the premier cost-reducer for the customers in your industry? Are you their premier revenue-increaser? If you want to be their premier grower, you will have to be one or the other, preferably both.

Locate, Identify, and Position Your Heavy Profit Contributors

Who are the customers on whom your growth depends? When you come right down to it, they are a remarkably small proportion of all your customers. If they total only 20 percent or so, you will be typical of most growth managers. Yet they are the 20 percent from whom as much as 80 percent of your profitable sales volume will flow.

If you are a brewer, fewer than 20 percent of all beer drinkers provide almost 80 percent of your industry's growth profits. If you are a pharmaceutical manufacturer, fewer than 20 percent of all prescribing physicians provide 80 percent or so of your industry's growth profits. If you are a retailer, fewer than 20 percent of all your shoppers provide 80 percent or so of your profits; fewer than 20 percent of all your goods do likewise.

We give these key customers a special name. We call them what they are: your heavy profit contributors. They are your major source of funds. Relatively few in number, they control your fate by their ability to select either your solution to their problems or someone else's and to invest premium funds in acquiring it.

Converting a sufficient number of heavy profit contributors to becoming investors in your solution is the crucial determinant of fast growth. If you can make the conversion, you can grow your business fast. If you cannot, you will not grow no matter what else you do well or how superbly well you do it. Since converting the heavy profit contributors — who are, after all, the heavy needers — is a marketing-dependent activity, you can see why marketing is the supercritical instrument of your growth.

A fast-growth business manager may be defined as a locator of his industry's heavy profit contributors, an identifier of their most critical problems and opportunities as well as the upper limits of the premium price boundaries they are willing to pay to benefit their needs, and a positioner of a product or service as the best investment in adding the value of the benefits they seek.

Locator, identifier, and positioner. Classical entrepreneurs have always been all three. A significant number of them have done these things intuitively. They have located a market by their own instinctive radar or they have been a part of it themselves. If you told them they were practicing market segmentation, they might not know what you meant. They have identified one of a market's most pressing problems or opportunities and put a premium price tag on the benefit they can offer in trade for it. If you told them they were practicing preferential positioning, they might not know what you meant.

Most of us who profess to be business growers need to know what these things mean. We need to know how, and why, in order to segment out the heavy profit contributors in our markets. We need to know how to zero in on their critical needs and how to put a premium value on benefiting them. We need to know how to position our business as their best investment adviser and how to position our products and systems as their best investments.

Distinguish Heavy Profit Contributors from Heavy Users

Heavy profit contributors are the heart of your business demand base. For all intents and purposes, they are your market. They are the customers you must coddle, communicate with, and convert into becoming loyal, consistent buyers at premium prices.

In order to keep a clear fix on your heavy profit contributors, you must avoid sloppy thinking about who they are. They may be largely composed of your heaviest users, customers whose need for your benefit values is large and ongoing. If they are predisposed to pay a premium price for their large volume purchases, they can be heavy profit contributors as well as heavy users. If not, they may be only low or medium profit contributors.

If heavy users demand deals and discounts or special terms for payment that delay your collection of receivables, if they require free goods or free complementary services to sweeten the act of purchase, or if they make purchase depend on favorable allowances, credits, or forgivenesses, they may not be highly profitable for you to serve no matter what price they are willing to pay.

When you are trying to grow a business, volume sales and increasing your share points in key markets may seem to be irresistible attractions. Resist them until you can distinguish between the heavy profit contributors on one hand and the users on the other who buy heavily but whose methods of doing business erode your profit. You cannot grow without volume. But volume without profit is an invitation to bankruptcy.

What can you do about heavy users who are not contributing heavily to profit? Three solutions are available. You can raise price to a superpremium level to pay for your subsidy of the purchases they are making now and thereby recover your full premium profit. Or you can assess a fee for currently free services that will be over and above the price for your product. Or, finally, you can tuck your product into a product-and-service system and post a premium price for the system.

Make Heavy Profit Contributors Your Heavy Investors

Heavy-profit-contributing customers can be defined in two ways. They are, as we have seen, your heavy needers. They are also your heavy benefiters. Customers who need to benefit heavily from doing business with you share certain characteristics that are not found among lighter needers. Some of these characteristics are generic. Heavy needers have to do business with someone — anyone, really — who offers a cost-effective solution to their problems or a similar means of seizing their opportunities. The four characteristics which foster their needs are the existence of a problem or opportunity, awareness that it is making a severe impact on their costs or revenues, a positive attitude toward reducing its costs or increasing its contribution to revenue, and recognition of a cost-effective remedy. This means that the remedy must be more effective than the existing process or function that is causing the problem and that it must make less of a negative contribution to cost or more of a positive contribution to profit.

There is a central assumption that underlies the generic characteristics of heavy needers. They must be able to quantify the financial impact of their problem or opportunity. If it has not been quantified, its contribution to profit will not be realized. As a result, assigning a value to it will be impossible. There can be no appreciation of a value if there is no quantification of it. Values have numbers. That gives them their worth. If your potentially heavy needers have not quantified the dollar value of their present profit problems and opportunities, you must do it with them. It is the first step in marketing.

How do you make your heavy contributors prefer to do business with you? Become their investment adviser, we have said. Offer them a premium value in hard, quantified dollars as their return on investment. Heal or enhance their bottom lines. They will make room for you at the top.

A heavy profit contributor is a heavy investor in your particular kind of return. This is a function of its quantity (how much you give) and its quality (how dependably you give, both in giving what you promise and in being on time). The handling of these two factors determines his evaluation of *opportunity*. This is what he really will buy: opportunity to strengthen the growth of his own businesses.

What do heavy profit contributors need the most? Give them the best opportunity to grow that they can obtain. What do heavy profit contributors fear the most? They are wary of missing the prime opportunity in favor of a lesser one. This incurs opportunity cost, the single most unaffordable cost to them, to you, and to anyone who wants to grow a business fast.

Market to Central Customer Processes

To be customer-sensitive means to be keen on the specific benefits that will enable you to convert generically heavy needers into your own heavy profit contributors. What are these specifics?

All heavy needers in the same market segment are markedly similar. Otherwise they would not be in the same segment. In truth, though, each one is different. If you know only their similarities, you will find it convenient to sell to them. If you know the individual differences of each of them, you will find it possible to market to them. Knowledge of the finite distinctions possessed by your heavy needers is the secret of converting them to heavy profit contributors.

The manager who understands the peculiarities of a heavy needer's business functions – the processes that contribute to his major costs and revenues – sits in the catbird seat of fast growth. He alone can know how to quantify how much a function is contributing to customer cost. He alone can prescribe the optimal remedy and quantify its contribution to cost reduction or revenue increases. He alone can value-base his price in relation to the contribution of his remedy and present it as measuring a premium value. He alone can ask for and receive acceptance as an exclusive source for supplying the remedy.

What are the central customer processes which can call forth your sensitivity? They are the process by which a customer's product or service is (1) developmentally engineered, (2) manufactured, (3) distributed, (4) sold, and (5) administered. These are his five major cost centers. Two of these functions, sales and distribution, are also revenue centers. What do you need to be sensitive about in relation to them?

Each central process is a cost generator. It takes money away from a customer's profits to staff it, pay for its operations, control them, and supervise their performance. If a process is well run, it will detract less from profit. If it is poorly run, it may detract more from profit than the sum of the values it creates. Either way, it can probably use help in two respects. One way is to reduce its current costs. Even a small reduction helps as long as the cost of implementing it is less than the reduction. A second way is to save new costs from being incurred. Here again, even small savings can help improve customer profit.

The two central business processes that are revenue generators as well as cost generators can be helped in one or both of two ways. The costs of selling and distribution can be reduced or new costs can be saved. Or their ability to produce revenues can be increased. Every new dollar of sales that can be developed from the same cost base will help improve a customer's profit. What about raising the cost base? New sales dollars that can come out of an increased cost base will also be welcome as long as the cost is less than the new revenues. If the cost base of sales and distribution can be reduced, the amount of money saved can be viewed as the equivalent of new sales dollars.

Central customer processes must be the major areas of your sensitivity because they are the pressure points of your customers' sensitivity about their own businesses. Customers go to sleep worrying about them. They wake up worrying about them. Some customers say that there are two kinds of costs: those that won't go away no matter what you do about them and those that get bigger by the very act of trying to reduce them. This is a cynical point of view. But it seems to express the persistent nature of costs and the tendency of many remedies to inflate them. It also underscores management's concern with costs. "You don't have to use the phrase 'rising costs,' " managers say. "It's needlessly repetitive. 'Costs' alone will do. They are always rising."

Reduce Customer Costs—But Pay Off by Increasing Customer Sales

Many customer companies are in a mature phase of their life cycles. Cost reduction is their key to immediate profit improvement. Their markets are mature. So are their product lines, which have become commodity businesses whose downward price elasticity is high and whose margins are correspondingly low. How can you help a customer like this improve profit? The best way, perhaps the only way, is to reduce some of his process costs that you can affect.

At the other end of the life cycle curve, the young end, is the growth customer. Sales are the key to his profit. Can you help him sell more? Can you help him sell at a higher price? Can you help reduce his cost of sales? Any improvement will help speed his growth. It will also speed your own growth along with his.

In this situation, customer sensitivity has an obvious meaning: you must be sensitive to a customer's needs to grow profitable sales revenues. If you do business with mature customers, your sensitivity may be screened by their more apparent need for cost reduction as the avenue to immediate improvement of their profit. But no matter what amount of cost reduction you can achieve, sooner or later new sales revenues must be brought on stream if a business is to survive, let alone grow. Your short-term strategy may have to be cost reduction. But your continuing relationship will have to be based on increasing sales dollars. Otherwise there may be no customer business remaining whose costs you can reduce.

We keep coming back to increased sales revenues as the touchstone for growth, both in your customer businesses and in your own. Why is that? There is no substitute for the capital infusions they provide. Growth is profit. Profit comes from sales. This is why all growth managers are sales-driven. And to be driven by sales means that you must be acutely sensitive about the principal factors that determine customer sales in the markets you serve.

When you are the acknowledged industry expert on growing your customers' sales, and you are accredited as such by your heavy-profit-contributing customers (not by your own generous acclaim), you will have the right to call yourself customer-sensitive. Knowledge, as Francis Bacon said, is power. Customer sales knowledge is the source of your business growth power.

Make Your Business Readable Backward

If you visualize your market as an inverted pyramid, the point on which it rests is the 20 percent of all your customers who contribute up to 80 percent or so of your profitable sales volume. This is a precarious base. It means you must capture all the heavy profit contributors you can persuade to do business with you. Once captured, they must be kept. Few in number though they are, they are your growth source. They are not just your market; they are your business. To build it, build them.

To say that you recognize this truism – which may suggest that you understand it intellectually, use it as an occasional yardstick in evaluating your own business actions, and recite it to others – is insufficient. Not only must you respect it. Your entire business must be conceived as a response to it. Someone looking at your business for the first time, or you yourself surveying it for the hundredth time, must be able to see the market through the business. The ultimate rationale for running the business the way it is run must be that this is the organization and these are the operating strategies that add the maximum values to your heavy profit contributors.

How do you make your business readable backward? By starting with the market and tracking it back to your business, the perception of who your heavy profit contributors are, what their principal values are, and how they prefer to receive them should all be instantly perceptible to a trained eye.

Market centering your major business operations around each significant segment of heavy profit contributors is one way. It makes mandatory your recognition of their primacy by building it into the very structure of your organization. Policy making is another way. How you choose to manage your business, in terms of your style and content, should reveal the customer values you must deliver. Your products and services must be revealing, also, since they are the delivery systems for customer values. By the same token, your product technology should be equally reflective of your markets. And, of course, your marketing strategies must vibrate with the same values as those of your heavy profit contributors.

In these ways, you let the market in. When you do, whose business are you managing anyway: theirs or yours? They have to be able to see it as *theirs* – as a business put together to serve them best. What better critique could you want from the sources of your growth? And how, then, should you see it? Virtually all company charters give lip service to relating business existence and service to customers. This usually means selling them something. Growth-business charters relate their objective of building fast profit making to *building customers*, not merely serving them. They go far beyond making a good product, shipping it on time, surrounding it with fair terms, charging a competitive price, and backing it with service and an actionable warranty. Growth businesses *teach* their heavy-profit-contributing customers how to use the products and services they market as growth tools, as instruments of speeded-up profits, and as improvers of customer bottom lines.

No doubt about it, a lot of money can be made by selling products to customers. But there is no doubt, either, that the fastest profit growth comes from building customer businesses and not just selling to them. If you operate this way, you will never have to worry about being customer-sensitive. It will be inescapable. Nor will you have to be concerned about whether your main profit sources are sensitive to your own existence, to the values you offer, and to their premium nature.

They will be. It will be messaged to them daily by their own fast growth, which will be the mirror image of yours.

PART III
The Four Fast-Growth Management Strategies

5
Put Profit Objectives First —
Not Volume

Your business is a money machine. To grow it, you must beef up the amount of money it brings down to the bottom line.

If your business needs to be increased in size in order to beef up its bottom line, increase it. If it needs to be shrunk, decrease it. If it needs to be made organizationally simplified or more complex; if it requires operational integration or decentralization and dispersion; if its product lines need to be diversified or, quite the opposite, rationalized according to more homogeneous criteria — whatever needs to be done to grow the earning power of the business should be done.

One standard, immutable, should prevail: Will it help the money machine bring more money down — and will it help more than any other strategy requiring a similar or lesser investment? If it will, do it. If not, turn away from it.

How much profit will it bring down? Will anything else bring down more? What is the most cost-effective way I can implement it?

These are the three questions that should always be on your mind. No strategy should be exempt from this sort of inquisition. Every strategy should be suspect. Loyalty to strategies, no matter how traditional or historically successful, is a mis-

placed virtue. Loyalty is required only to objectives. As far as
strategies are concerned, if a strategy grows your business
best, implement it.

Begin with Profits—Don't End with Them

For a slow-growth business, profits are a residue. They are
the leftovers after the costs that helped generate them are paid
off.

As a fast-growth business manager, you must look at profits
in a different way. Instead of being what is left, profits are
what you must start with: the up-front growth objective of
your business. They are your beginning point, not the end.
From the start, they define the worthwhileness of your enterprise as a growth medium. Every strategy must be designed to
achieve them as whole as possible, to avoid diluting them and
to increase the chance that they will be gathered in.

When you regard profit as what you start with, managing a
business becomes single-purpose: to end with what you start
with. At the very outset, this imposes two constraints on how
the business is managed. First, it forces you to concentrate on
the smallest number of strategies that will bring home the
original profit objective. Fewer strategies are easier to manage, which helps you to optimize their efficiency. Fewer may
also be cheaper, helping you to keep down the cost of the means
of profit making. Second, it encourages you to seek the least
expensive strategies, thereby avoiding overengineering, over-
staffing, and overstrategizing.

Starting with profits is no guarantee that you will end with
them. But it does help guarantee that the efficiency rate of
going after them will be kept high and the cost base of pursu-
ing them will be kept low. Nothing can be more conducive to
growth profits than that.

Adopt the Philosophies of Financial Growth

Managing a growth business means running a big profit
maker – not necessarily a big volume mover or a big market-

share owner but an accumulator of significant incremental earnings. The size of the increments determines the rate of your business growth. Managing for growth is managing for increments.

Growth profits are the ultimate added values that can be brought into your business. Added people values in the form of skill and talent resources, added technological resources in the form of new sciences or new laboratory facilities, added manufacturing capacity, added marketing reach—all are means to the end of added profit values. In themselves, they represent costs of growth. A more dignified name for them, but a name that implies no less expense, is strategies.

Financial objectives that reflect superior incremental profits are the heart of your growth business. They are at one and the same time the reason for its existence, the challenge of its mission, and the proof of its accomplishment. One more thing: They are also the source of the fun of managing for growth because they allow you to measure your performance.

Because of this obsession with adding incremental profits, growth managers are often criticized for managing by the numbers. It makes them sound mechanistic, robotlike, inhumane. But no manager really manages numbers. The numbers that represent growth are the results of a small cluster of concepts. These are what business growers manage. This makes them the philosophers of growth, not its mechanics.

What are the chief philosophies of business financial growth? There are five of them. They can be summarized in this way:

1. Maximize the margins of growth.

2. Minimize the costs of growth.

3. Concentrate on marketing the main product sources of profit contribution to the main growth markets.

4. Control the percentage of profit on sales and the investment turnover.

5. Institutionalize the return-on-investment approach to calculating growth.

Use the Sales-But Growth Strategy

Taking a business on to superior growth in a foreshortened time is a sales-driven strategy. More accurately, it should probably be called a sales-but strategy. Emphatically, your sales must turn over rapidly if fast growth is to be attained. But sales must be conditioned by costs. Sales must be modified by margins. Sales must be managed in terms of profit contribution. Yes, sales . . . *but* watch their costs, their margins, and their profit contribution. These are the three rules of the road for driving a business up the profit curve.

RULE ONE: WATCH YOUR COSTS

Accountants define fixed costs as time costs. They increase or, less often, decrease over time. A monthly fixed cost of $X will amount to $3X at the end of three months regardless of whether your sales grow, stagnate, or decline. For this reason, fast-growth managers define fixed costs as profit-eaters.

To grow fast – that is, to condense the months or years it takes for you to drive a business to its full potential – the accumulation of costs over time must be kept to a minimum. The injunction to watch out for a buildup of fixed costs can be translated into two components. First, keep your overhead costs as low as possible. Second, keep the time frames within which you are committed to pay them as long as possible. In other words, pay out small and pay out long.

If keeping fixed costs down is such a good idea, why is it so universally ignored in practice? Fixed costs are insidious. They creep in everywhere, eroding business growth. Some of them are necessary to provide the foundation for growth. Many are not. Growth management is a 24-hour-a-day vigil against the proliferation of fixed costs. If the vigil is relaxed, costs can grow faster than profits.

One of the greatest nullifiers of profit growth is unabsorbed fixed cost. When profits cannot be grown faster than the costs that have been run up to generate them, a business is being managed for its creditors. Rule one in growing a business is therefore, watch your costs.

An important part of that rule is not to play games between

fixed and variable costs. Variable costs used to be looked on as the opposite of costs that were fixed. But as soon as a business is managed for fast growth, this alleged relationship is revealed to be a fable. It is true, of course, that variable costs can rise and fall as the number of units sold increases and decreases. Nonetheless, variable costs have a fixed relationship to selling price. This makes them price-dependent. As growth comes on strong, you will have to endure them as if they were indeed the same as fixed.

RULE TWO: WATCH YOUR MARGINS

When your variable costs are subtracted from sales, the value that remains is contribution margin. This is the revenue flow that contributes first to absorbing fixed costs and then to profit. Contribution margin is the mother of your growth profits. Either they come into being here or they will not exist. Accordingly, the product lines that produce the greatest contribution margins should be revered. They are your wellsprings of growth.

Rule two in growing a business is therefore, watch your margins. Are they growing? Are they growing fast enough? Are they growing steadily and progressively? Is their source changing? If one product line's contribution margin is showing signs of shrinking—in other words, if the life cycle is catching up with it—do you have replacement contribution you can begin to factor into your growth plan?

The concept of contribution margin can be seen in Table 1 as it would appear in operating statement terms. In Table 2, contribution margin is shown according to product line correlation, and in Table 3 sales are correlated with a line's product-by-product contribution.

The effects of volume on your contribution margin and the effects of contribution margin on costs can be illustrated by a simple example. Assume that your business is burdened by $30 million in fixed costs. At zero sales, contribution margin will also be zero. The business will show a loss of exactly $30 million.

The loss will decline up through breakeven, which occurs at

Table 1. Contribution margin in operating statement terms.

Sales (50,000 units @ $80)	$4,000,000	100.0 %
Cost of goods manufactured and sold:		
Variable manufacturing costs		
(50,000 units @ $10)	500,000	12.5
Manufacturing contribution margin	3,500,000	87.5 %
Selling and administrative expense:		
Variable selling and administrative		
expenses (50,000 units @ $5)	250,000	6.25
Contribution margin	$3,250,000	81.25%

Table 2. Contribution margin by product line.

	Total	A	B	C	D
Number of units sold	396,000	32,000	100,000	84,000	180,000
Selling price per unit	$14.80AV	$15.00	$8.00	$16.00	$18.00
Variable manufacturing cost*	6.06AV	9.80	4.90	9.60	4.40
Variable selling and					
administrative expense	.57AV	1.00	.18	1.00	.50
Contribution margin	$8.17AV	$4.20	$2.92	$5.40	$13.10
Total fixed costs	$1,726,000				

NOTE: AV = average of product lines
*Materials, factory supplies, labor, other variable costs.

Table 3. Contribution margin in relation to sales.

Product Line	% Total Sales	% Product Line Contribution Margin on Sales	% Product Line Contribution Margin to Total
A	8.2	27.9	4.1
B	13.6	36.5	9.0
C	22.9	33.8	14.0
D	55.3	72.8	72.9
Total	100.0	52.2*	100.0

*Average contribution margin on total sales.

about 35 million units of sales. From breakeven on, the business makes money. Subsequent dollars of contribution margin will begin to flow to the bottom line. This is profit. But it is not necessarily what we think of as growth.

Once beyond breakeven, the differences between normal incremental growth and fast growth become dramatic. At a normal rate of growth—what might be called adequate—the business can sell 5 million units. At this volume, contribution margin will be $50 million. By subtracting fixed costs of $30 million, we arrive at a profit of $20 million. But if fast growth management can step up sales by another 2 million units, contribution margin can increase to $70 million and profit will rise to $40 million—double the amount achieved by the sale of 5 million units. If the incremental cost of obtaining these new profit dollars is acceptable, it can be a good buy.

Operating profit relies on contribution margin. What does contribution margin rely on? Given two businesses in the same industry with similar fixed costs, the business that is managed to keep down variable costs will be more profitable.

The same principle can be expressed in another, more dynamic way. All sales must be bought. Variable costs, which are essentially sales costs, are the price of sales. *Profit comes from minimizing the cost of maximizing sales.* The most cost-efficient sales producer wins the profit prize.

RULE THREE: WATCH YOUR PROFIT CONTRIBUTION

A single-product, single-market business has a single source of profit contribution. If it expands to serve multiple markets, it will have multiple sources of contribution. Contribution per market will be the key factor in managing the business for growth. Analyzing the needs of its heavy-profit-contributing markets and heavying up the allocation of the assets of the business to benefit these markets in a preemptive manner become the principal operating strategy for growth.

A multiproduct business presents a similar problem in assessing and managing the sources of its profit contribution. No matter how many products the business sells, or how many markets the products serve, the major profit contribution will always be found to come from a few products sold to a small number of markets. This is the 80-20 rule in action. It greatly simplifies the problem of managing growth; indeed, it makes growth possible in a multiproduct, multimarket company. If as much as 80 percent of profit contribution can come from as little as 20 percent of all products sold and all markets sold to, growth management means concentrating on big-winner products bought by the heaviest-profit-contributing markets.

No matter how many sources of profit contribution your business may have, its growth base will be small since its sources of major profit must be few. This makes growth precarious: so much depends on so few contributors. But it also makes growth possible. It takes an extraordinary dedication of management skill, motivation, and resources to make a business grow fast. There is never enough to go around. Fortunately, it does not have to go around everything.

Because your growth sources are at a minimum, they are at a premium. This means they should be safeguarded like the crown jewels they are. They should be analyzed so they are exceedingly well known. They should be funded for aggressive marketing. They should be managed entrepreneurially so they can maximize revenues and throw off their full potential contribution before their growth curves flatten out into maturity.

Live by the Growth Diagnostic Ratios

There are two major types of growth tests you can apply to your business. One type can be called *profitability tests*. They consist of four ratios which reveal profit, income, and return. The second type can be called *activity tests*. They consist of ratios which reveal the levels of sales in relation to inventory, receivables, and assets. These ratios should be monitored in an ongoing, real-time manner to keep an eye on how your growth is progressing and what its costs and rewards are.

Profitability ratios

Gross profit ratio	=	Gross profit ÷ Sales
Net income to sales	=	Net income ÷ Sales
Percent profit on sales	=	Net profit ÷ Sales
Return on investment (ROI)	=	Net income ÷ Total assets

Activity ratios

Inventory turnover	=	Sales ÷ Inventory
Day's sales in inventory	=	365 Days ÷ Inventory turnover
Accounts receivable turnover	=	Credit Sales ÷ Accounts receivable
Collection period (days)	=	365 Days ÷ Accounts receivable turnover
Investment turnover	=	Net sales ÷ Total investment

If you have trouble keeping an eye — or even both eyes — on so many indicators, concentrate on two: percent profit on sales and investment turnover. If your growth is to be vigorous, you will have to keep them both high.

PERCENT PROFIT ON SALES

Profit as a percentage of sales is an index of how well you are adjusting the critical mix between the sales volume of a product line and the costs of producing it.

Percent profit on sales for a product line can be calculated by dividing net profit (contribution to profit) by sales:

$$\frac{\text{Net profit}}{\text{Sales}} = \text{Percent profit on sales}$$

The answer to the question, "Are you growing the business?" is not "Yes, I am growing sales." In terms of volume or market share, sales by itself is a meaningless index. The only viable answer is, "Yes, I am growing our profit as a percentage of sales." This says two things. The business is being grown. Its growth is being managed.

INVESTMENT TURNOVER

Your business represents an investment. The bet of fast-growth management is that your profits can greatly exceed it. The central issue of growing a business can be stated in these terms: How can I get my capital investment to circulate faster?

Capital investment starts with cash. Capital circulation starts with causing your cash funds to flow into inventory. Capital circulation continues with flowing these funds from inventories into receivables. This is the first key step in adding to the magnitude of your original funds. The reason for its impact is simple. Inventories are valued at cost but receivables are valued at sales. The difference between them is your gross profit.

Capital circulation concludes its turnover when funds flow from receivables to cash – when you make a collection. At this point, the amount of initial capital funds invested in your business has increased. Growth has taken place, as it will again with each new turnover. Maximizing your investment turnover is therefore a principal fast-growth strategy.

Investment turnover can be calculated by dividing net sales by total investment, which is the same as dividing by total assets:

$$\frac{\text{Net sales}}{\text{Total investment}} = \text{Percent investment turnover}$$

The role of increasing sales is paramount in maximizing the turnover of your invested capital. Fast-growth management is primarily sales-growth management. Yet sales growth must always be modified by the role of reducing or at least limiting the total operating investment in the business all the while sales are being increased. Growth is not simply sales. Growth is cost-effective sales. Fast-growth management is not simply selling. Fast growth is the end result of selling up while investing down. In short, managing profit contribution requires you to drive your business with both hands – sales and investment – on the wheel.

Take an ROI Approach to Calculating Growth

The basic return-on-investment (ROI) formula for calculating growth divides profit contribution by the amount of funds you have invested in operations. In a fast-growing business, an expanded formula for calculating and measuring profitability can be more useful. It can help suggest ways to continue to improve profitability by enabling you to focus on improving turnover. Turnover reflects both options for growth: the value of increasing sales and the value of decreasing the investment in operating assets. The expanded formula looks like this:

$$\text{Percent profit on sales} \times \text{Turnover rate}$$

or

$$\frac{\text{Net operating profit}}{\text{Sales}} \times \frac{\text{Sales}}{\text{Total funds invested}}$$

By using this ROI formula, you will be able to make any one of three calculations in order to analyze the basis for your business growth:

1. The business is growing because both its percent profit on sales and its turnover rate are higher.

2. The business is growing because its percent profit on sales is higher even though turnover is lower. Growth can be stepped up additionally by increasing turnover.

3. The business is growing because its turnover rate is higher even though percent profit on sales is lower. Growth can be stepped up additionally by increasing percent profit on sales.

Because investments must be made today for returns on them that may not accrue until some future time, the present value of future returns must always be considered. The objective of investing is not merely to make money. It is to make the most money.

Since investment and return generally occur in different time frames, an equivalent basis must be used to determine whether the most money is in fact being made. Present investment dollars have to be placed on a future dollar scale of values by compounding them; that is, by computing the compound amount of a present investment.

A present investment of $100 that can earn 10 percent interest compounded annually will return $121 at the end of two years. Any competitive investment opportunity that is expected to yield less than $121 in two years may therefore be unacceptable because it is not equivalent to $100 today. Any investment that will return $121 makes money. If it returns more than that, it may be able to make the most money.

Play the Game—Don't Just Settle for the Name

Fast-growth managers come to work every morning dedicated to the proposition that profit is the name of the game. Sales are the drivewheel of profit. So they concentrate on moving the goods out the shipping room door.

The indicators to watch revolve around sales. Are costs being kept minimal? Are margins being maximized? Is profit contribution being carefully watched on a product-by-product, product-line-by-product-line basis in every market? Are the big-winner products that make the greatest profit contribution being pushed most aggressively? Are they the ones that are supported by the most sizable appropriations for advertising and sales promotion? Are they the ones that earn the highest commissions for the sales force?

Keeping these questions in mind, and answering them, is what managing a growth business is all about. It is the game of which profit is the name.

6

Position Your Products
as Brands —
Not Commodities

Fast growth is the result of a stream of premium profits flowing into your business. Premium profits are themselves the result of premium unit prices. The growth equation is simple: premium unit price multiplied by volume. But how can premium price be obtained? The answer is by *branding* your business so that it is perceived by its market as offering a premium value.

Branding — that is, adding perceived premium value — is the key to commanding premium price. It is the single most crucial attribute of any business that wants to grow. Unless a business is branded, preferably at its inception, it will not be able to command a premium unit price. Its price will be cost-based, not value-based. It will, inevitably, be a slow-growth or no-growth commodity business.

Entrepreneurial businesses that march quickly up the growth curve have something distinctive going for them. They have won from their markets the attribution of delivering an added value. Sometimes the market will call the added value new, sometimes it will be called different or distinctive. At other times it will be described as unique, better, or best. Whatever the words that are used, one thing is clear. The value that is perceived is worth a high price because, no matter how high the price, the value is understood to be even higher.

Growth businesses are distinguished businesses. They are distinguished by a differentiating factor that permits their user benefit to be perceived as worthy of a premium price. This differentiating factor is their premium. It enables them to command a premium in return.

The commanding factor that differentiates a business from its competitors in this way is its brand. A business whose products or services are perceived as meriting premium price is a branded business: branded with the stamp of delivering an added value to the user.

Brand the Business as Your First Management Act

A brand, as the term is used in this context, is not a product name or trademark. It is not created by advertising and sales. They are its principal vehicles; it is delivered by them. Brands are created — that is, they are positioned — by business managers to exist in the perceptions of their markets. Managers position brands; markets perceive them. The market's perception is the manager's sole valid test of his positioning skill.

What happens when a manager possesses insufficient positioning skill? To ask the same question in another way, what is the penalty for being brand-deficient? The net result is a commodity business, one that cannot command a premium price, or cannot command it for long, *in spite of the fact that it may possess technical superiority.*

Commodity products are the curse of fast-growth businesses. True, their volume can often be increased under growth pressure. Their share of market can be expanded. The cost-effectiveness of their operations can be improved. But unless their price can be increased so that profit per unit can be maximized, they will not support superior profit growth.

It is essential that you make your first act as a fast-growth manager the construction of a branded position for your business. The second act must be to create a marketing thrust that will enable the business to be perceived as adding a superior value to its users.

Brand User Value—Not Product Performance

What is the essence of branding? It is embodied in one injunction: *Add superior value to your product's users, not just to your product.*

Users, not products, are the proper targets of branding. Only users can perceive value. A product may possess superior technical value. But if its market does not perceive it, the value will not exist as far as the market is concerned. It still exists for the design engineers who have built it into the product. But alas, they only make; they do not buy.

The values that markets perceive are the benefits that they can get out of a product, not the features and characteristics that its engineers have put into it. Made better must mean that the product benefits better, or quality will not be worth its cost.

The act of engineering quality into a product is its dearest expenditure. Quality comes high. Superior quality comes highest. The expenditure for quality manufacture or quality performance will be either an unrecoverable cost or an investment on which a greater return can be received. What determines which way it will go? The market is the decision maker. It can sting you with an unrecoverable cost if your quality inputs do not yield what it regards as quality outputs. On the other hand, it can return a hundredfold every dollar you invest in quality if its user value is superior.

The brandability of user value is not an argument for inferior products. It is an appeal for superior user value as the objective of every dollar's commitment to product design, engineering, manufacturing, or marketing.

Technically inferior products can and do win market perception as conveyors of superior user value. Conversely, technically superior products can and do fail. Nowhere is this paradox clearer than in the data processing and automobile industries.

THE IBM/UNIVAC CASE

In the 1950s Univac was broadly acknowledged to possess technical superiority in the computer business. IBM was not. Yet a generation later IBM was to have $50 billion worth of computer systems in place while Univac had one-tenth that amount. What happened?

Of all the acknowledgers of Univac's technical superiority, Univac was the proudest. Accordingly, it sold product quality. It translated quality into a product output, speed. It expressed speed of access to the data its processing systems created in units called nanoseconds, or billionths of a second. IBM could not match Univac's product performance. With a perceived mix of product inferiority, some parity, and some unavailability, IBM was forced to sell a different kind of quality: the quality of a user input, improved profit. It expressed profit in dollars delivered to the user's bottom line from either new sales revenues gained by computerized operations or costs saved or reduced.

Superior bottom lines (greater profits) have proved to be a more compelling benefit than superior computer performance (fewer nanoseconds). By their purchase decisions, customers have said that their preference for buying improved balance sheets for their own businesses exceeds their interest in buying the improved product of someone else's business.

Univac attempted to brand its product on the basis of scientific supremacy. It failed. IBM succeeded in branding its solution as the standard solution to the common user problem of insufficient profit. Univac spent multiple millions of dollars in perfecting the technology of making machines. IBM invested multiple millions of dollars in perfecting a different technology: the knowledge of how its users make profit and how their profits can be improved by the application of computer technology.

THE CADILLAC/LINCOLN CASE

If Cadillac is substituted for IBM and Lincoln for Univac, the two cases are almost identical. In the 1960s Lincoln was acknowledged by automotive experts to possess technical superiority. Cadillac was not. Yet Cadillac came to lead Lincoln by 6.5 to 1 in fine car sales.

Like Univac, Lincoln sold product quality. It translated

quality into product performance and construction features. Cadillac sold another kind of quality, the improved financial features that would occur in an owner's budget from the greater return on a Cadillac's original investment. The return became available on resale. Cadillac expressed the difference between its car and Lincoln as this net difference in dollars received at trade-in.

For Cadillac, superior return on investment has proved to be a more compelling benefit than superior automotive engineering. By their purchase decisions, customers have made it clear that their preference for buying improved budgets exceeds their interest in buying an improved automobile.

Lincoln attempted to brand its product on the basis of engineering superiority. It failed. Cadillac succeeded in branding its solution as the standard solution to the common car owner problem of rationalizing the purchase of a fine car. Lincoln spent multiple millions of dollars in perfecting the technology of making machines. Cadillac invested multiple millions of dollars in perfecting a different technology: the knowledge of how its owners make purchase decisions and how they can be made comfortable with a major purchase that is positioned as a returnable investment.

What is the common denominator in these two cases? Knowledge of users is the touchstone to branding. If you know your users, you can know what they hold to represent superior value and you can build to match it. When your users' perceptions of superior value coincide with your engineers' perceptions, you will be doubly blessed. But that does not require management. What does? When your users' perceptions and your engineers' perceptions disagree, you will have to manage to make the user supreme if you want your business to achieve fast growth.

Avoid the Perfect Product

Growth managers must avoid product perfection like the snare and delusion it is. To quest for it and not find it can destroy your resource base, especially time. To quest for it and find it can be even worse. It can destroy your business growth.

Product perfection is the antagonist of growth. Its costs add to price, perhaps beyond the point of recovery. Even worse, its very existence can cripple marketing. Given the achievement of a high degree of perfection, it is a rare manager who can resist the temptation to sell from it. Under the masquerade of quality, the product will be advertised and sold on the basis of perfect features, perfect characteristics, perfect benefits. The product will proclaim itself rather than being proclaimed by its market. It will feature itself rather than its users' added values. It will, in short, product-orient its selling process rather than market-orient it.

"We are the quality supplier." Or "We are the quality leader in the industry." These are positioning platforms to beware of. They represent a business talking to itself and to its competitors, not to its market. They reflect a management style that believes products to be the sources of growth. Products grow only costs. Markets grow businesses because markets are where the money is.

To grow a business fast, what a manager requires is not a perfect product but a perfect matchup between the market's need for benefits from the product and the product's capability for yielding those benefits. In other words, growth depends more on perfected marketing than on perfected products.

Can a less-than-perfect product be branded? It can; indeed it must be branded if it is to provide the source of quickened growth. Less-than-perfect products must meet two criteria.

1. They must possess positive characteristics that will permit a market to derive its single most critical benefit from them in the easiest, most abundant manner.

2. They must not possess negative characteristics that will prevent a market from deriving its single most critical benefit from them, or that will dilute the satisfaction it affords or cause it to be priced higher than its value.

Beyond these two criteria, little else matters in the way markets perceive products. They are the essentials. The first is a product that works best. It delivers maximum incremental value. Second, its price is fair. Even though it may be high, its perceived value is even higher.

Brand Your Sales Force

At the same time that commodity-product salesmen are attempting to preserve low margins or regain list price, branded-product salesmen are across the street commanding premium prices based on the value they can add to customer businesses. The premium they command is not a bonus based on superior construction characteristics or performance benefits of their product. Nor is it due to their own superior ability to solve customer problems. For a branded-product salesman, premium price is the natural reward for conferring a premium value on customers.

How do you brand your sales force? These five strategies will help get you there.

1. *Positioning as profit improvers.* Branded sales forces take a position with their customers as being improvers of customer profit. Don't think of me as a purveyor of goods and services, they say. Regard me as someone who is in your employ without being on your payroll, who comes into your business with proposals to help increase your profit, and who works with your people to implement each proposal so that the profit it promises will be achieved. When you see me, say to yourself, "Here comes someone who helps me grow my business."

2. *Interacting as a consultant.* Branded sales forces relate to customers as their consultants in profit improvement, not as product vendors. They play a consultative role because, just as product movement is the province of vendors, counseling on using products to lower customer costs and increase customer sales is the province of consultants. Only consultants possess the necessary up-front information on a customer's business to sell in this way. Only consultants receive continuing infusions of information from a customer so they can go on selling consultatively.

3. *Ruling out debate on product merits.* Branded sales forces avoid selling product features and benefits. They try to prevent

a feature-by-feature, benefit-by-benefit comparison of their products with competitive offerings. They attempt to create acceptance for what their products can do for a customer's bottom line rather than what they are made of or what they do in a customer's business functions or processes in which they are installed. They sell the ultimate benefit: new profits for the customer. They do not allow themselves to be trapped into putting forth or defending intermediate or contributory benefits of a construction or operating nature. They concentrate on the end result. Their proposal asks, "Do you want this amount of new profit?" instead of "Do you want this product?"

4. *Appropriating the industry standard of value.* Branded sales forces institutionalize the amounts of profit by which they improve customer businesses as the industry standard. In this way, they establish themselves as bearers of the official yardstick which determines superior performance. Our ability to improve profit is the standard of performance in your industry, they say. This is the reason you must do business with us. In order to compete against us, another company must be able to exceed our standard . . . not just once or twice, but consistently. If and when it does, it will set the new standard. But until that happens, the standard is ours. Everyone else must be measured against us, unfavorably.

5. *Selling systems.* Branded sales forces frequently package several products and product-related services into a single unit called a system. Systems are designed to solve more comprehensive customer problems than single products and to justify a higher price based on their higher value in doing so. Systems are also a competitive weapon. They prevent gaps in the way customer problems are solved through which a rival source can gain entry as an alternate supplier and thereafter broaden its penetration toehold to become the supplier of choice. Perhaps the essential value of selling systems is the proof they furnish of how well a sales force knows the business problems and opportunities of the customer and can custom-tailor solutions to them. This is the crux of branding.

In a commodity product business, the role of the sales function is traditional. The sales force mission is to sell product.

Since commodity products can bear only small margins, the sales force charge is more accurately expressed this way: Sell volume.

The role of a branded sales function is significantly different. Branded sales forces prescribe and install product, but they never sell product. Instead, they use their sales position to add profit to their customer businesses. They act as customer profit-improvers, not bidders, order writers, deliverymen, or service representatives. Their product is not the physical, tangible item manufactured by their company. It is the new, improved profits they are able to supply to their accounts.

The product of every branded sales force is customer profit. This is what the business sells to its markets. This is what customer accounts actually buy: the improved profit that comes from dealing with a branded sales force.

How do you brand your sales force? You teach it how to sell the contribution that your product can make to improve customer profit. You teach it to quantify the contribution in dollar terms. Added value for the user in terms of improved profit becomes the sales force's stock in trade. Accordingly, it becomes their brand.

Brand Your Advertising

Advertising is a multiplier. It multiplies the distribution of a brand's ultimate benefit, its ability to earn new profits for its customers. For consumer products, advertising is the retailer's guidebook to profit improvement. It is also the "sales force" that calls on end users. It positions the brand as its product category's standard of value. It puts forth consultative spokesmen who can interact with customers: Betty Crocker, the Jolly Green Giant, Colonel Sanders, and the rest. They rule out debate on product merits.

Professional service businesses and high technology companies should advertise in pretty much the same way as consumer brand advertisers. High technology companies and manufacturers of industrial products such as valves, tanks, pumps, and scales require variations on the consumer theme. Their best consultative spokesman is a top-level customer. Positioning a product system as the industry standard can best be accomplished by testimonial case histories which prove its profit-improving achievement.

For capital-intensive industrial companies, advertising is the sales force complement. It has two objectives. The first objective is to help position the sales force by generating customer awareness of its consultative, profit-improving mission and by creating positive customer attitudes toward its ability to accomplish the profit mission. Advertising's second objective is to make the calls on class B and C accounts, the light profit contributors, that are cost-ineffective for the sales force to deal with in person.

THE IBM EXAMPLE

IBM, a fast-growth company, uses advertising to position the branded nature of its business. The presidents of customer companies testify to the results they have obtained for their businesses because they engaged the services of IBM. In case history scenarios, they bear witness to results such as these:

"At Black & Decker, we gained $15 million in sales through forecasting with our on-line data base."

"At Heinz U.S.A., we increased order entry productivity by 75 percent and saved $200,000 with distributed processing."

Each of these customers bought the same product from IBM: ostensibly a System/370 data processor but actually a quantified profit improvement. In other words, they bought new dollars. Black & Decker gained 15 million new dollars by reducing sales lost by unavailability of merchandise. At the same time, the IBM forecasting system saved another $1 million a year in computing costs and helped increase employee productivity by 24 percent. These are essentially bonuses added to the $15 million sales gain.

Heinz began to collect 200,000 new dollars from improved operating efficiency as soon as it went on line with its IBM system. Then, on a daily basis, it benefited from a 75 percent increase in average orders entered per employee. These are the branded benefits from dealing with IBM. How can the added value of the benefits be expressed? The market's answers to two questions tell the story.

All computer companies make data processing systems. What is the value added by IBM? As far as the market is concerned, IBM does not make computers. IBM makes customer companies more profitable. Improved customer profit is its product. What is the specific added value of IBM's product? IBM's product is more bottom-line dollars for a customer's balance sheet than any other data processor can provide or may believably promise. When customers buy from IBM, they buy what IBM persuades them to buy: results that they can take to the bank. The dollars delivered by IBM become the data processing market's standard value. All other computer companies must compete against it. Until they improve on it, IBM remains the standard.

Through creating perceptions of unique added value, a branded sales and advertising message becomes the product in the awareness of the market. It is the added value that is bought, not the physical product itself. Preference for the added value precedes acquisition of the product. Acceptance of the added value as a premium predisposes acceptance of a premium price. These are the two objectives of marketing. Their net effect is called branding.

To Be Branded, Price Like a Brand

To grow a business fast, the marketing process must be employed like a lever. Preference before purchase must be obtained at the highest level, that of insistence. Acceptance of a product's added value is critical if it is to merit the highest price. When marketing is professionally managed as a growth tool, these are its outcomes. They are the standards for marketing performance in a growth business because they are the standards for branding the business.

The fair price of a brand is dear. A brand possesses the right to command a premium price because of its perceived worth to its users, not because of any intrinsic worth of its components or ingredients. Premium price is a brand's birthright. It is conferred on brands as their market's reward for delivering a premium value.

What does a pricing premium consist of? The premium, or the margin conferred by branding, should be the leadership price. It should lead the industry. There is no sense in making and marketing a brandable product if it cannot be its industry's price leader.

A second question to consider is, What constitutes leadership? One answer is simply the highest price in the industry. That should be a brand's minimum requirement. In practice, most brands should be priced between 20 and 30 percent higher than the nearest competition. This is the margin within which premium profits can be grown.

If brand pricing at these levels of supremacy is to be marketable, the user value of a brand must be perceived as being even higher. As long as the brand's premium value is perceived to exceed its premium price, a positive value-to-price relationship can exist. This will insure fast-growth sales.

Expressed as a formula, a brand's value-to-price relationship can be stated like this:

$$PPV > PP$$

In other words, a brand's perceived premium value (PPV) must exceed its premium price (PP). In theory, at least, there is no fixed upper limit on price except the value that is attributed to the brand. If price exceeds it or competition shrinks the gap between your brand's value and its price, the brand will appear to be overpriced. In relation to user value, it will be. This is true no matter how high the product's engineered value may be or how low you set price.

Over and above providing growth profits, premium price serves an additional purpose. It defines a brand as being branded. It validates the market's perception that a premium value is obtainable. In the same way that value justifies price, price testifies to the existence of value. This two-way interlocking relationship is a brand's greatest strength. It safeguards the brand from user debate on its construction or performance merits. It also protects the brand from competitive products that claim an ability to deliver equal or higher value at a lower price.

Brand pricing at premium levels serves four functions of fast business growth: It is a premium profit generator, a product positioner, a market-share penetrator, and a competitive defender. It is the cause as much as the end effect of branding.

7
Use Marketing for Leverage — Not Engineering

Growth at a faster than average rate requires leverage — something to give growth an upward thrust and to keep upward pressure on it to make sure it continues to rise. There are only two possible levers to consider. One is product technology, which includes research and development, engineering, and manufacturing. The other is marketing technology, which includes sales, advertising, pricing, and market analysis.

Except for a few rare instances, choosing product technology as a growth lever will condemn a business to slow growth or no growth. The choice of marketing technology will not guarantee fast growth. Rapid acceleration of your profit and cash flow cannot, however, dependably take place without it.

What is marketing's magic touch? Product technologies operate on making things better. Market technologies operate on benefiting customers better. While it is something of an oversimplification to separate them in this way, there is no doubt that moving markets is the prerequisite to moving products; that making products capable of delivering better benefits is the customer's definition of better; and that the heavy profit contributors in a market are every product's principal source of revenues and earnings.

Instill Added Values in Market Minds

Added value can be conferred on users from three sources. Sometimes, but not often, it is derived directly from the technical superiority of a product. The product's added performance value can be translated one-for-one as its user's added value. More frequently, added user value does not come from products but is the direct result of their marketing. This is value added by marketing—the result of using marketing as it should be used, to create perceptions of unique added value regardless of whether product performance values are superior or not.

The third source of added value is a combination of product technology and marketing. When the two generators of worth can be harnessed together in this way growth can receive its greatest impetus. In the absence of this ideal blend, the marketing component is the only one that can create a branded business position by itself. Why is technical superiority unmarketable in and of itself? No business can be based entirely on added scientific values if they are not transformed into user values that can be perceived as uniquely superior.

A better mousetrap by itself is not the basis for a growth business. More cost-effective rodent control may be. The mousetrap is patentable but not brandable. The mousetrap user's benefit, cost-effective rodent control, is not patentable. But it is marketable. It is therefore the sole aspect of the business that can be branded. If an attempt is made to brand the mousetrap instead of the user's benefit, there will be no superior value. Instead, there will be a superior inventory of mousetraps.

Branding is the sine qua non of a growth business. This suggests where branding a fast-growing business takes place. It does not occur in the laboratory, although superior technical processes, components, or ingredients may originate there. It does not occur in product engineering or manufacturing in spite of zero defects. It occurs only in the perceptions of a market. What puts those perceptions there? The only answer is marketing, the sum total of all the advertising and sales impressions that touch on user awareness.

Avoid the Machinist's Trap

Putting too much machined value into a product has the same effect as putting in too little—with one exception. Too much machined value costs more than too little. The added cost may not be recoverable through premium pricing, either in whole or in part. Small to nonexistent margins result. Growth is made impossible.

Falling into the machinist's trap can take two forms. A product can have excess quality—perhaps excess qualities is a better way to say it. Or it can have an excess of the wrong qualities, wrong in terms of what its market prefers and is willing to pay a premium for. Too many qualities or too many wrong qualities depress demand in three ways. A critical use value that a market wants may be lost in the shuffle. It may simply be obscured in a flurry of other alleged benefits, denying the product a precise positioning. Or the critical value may not be there at all, making the product's positioning inept. Finally, a mix of alternate values may cause a net positioning that is incorrect on balance for its market's requirements.

No product can be marketed for what it is not. A machinist kind of product cannot even be marketed for what it is: a disharmonious matchup with market preference. If you want to grow a business fast, you must not be at the mercy of your machinists. You and your people must recognize that you are all at the mercy of your market. Since the market's judgment on product value will be a product's eventual benediction or its curse, growth-product planning must start at the same point where it will inevitably end: with your perception of what constitutes superior value for the end user.

You may not deliberately overmachine. But many companies, especially high technology manufacturers, deliberately underresearch their markets. Inside wizardry rather than outside perception is allowed to determine what ingredients or components will go into a product and therefore what benefits will come out of it. What goes in is often the epitome of the state of the art: the greatest number of the most highly advanced product features that can be packed in. Or, in other words, perfect products which will have imperfect sales curves.

Translate "Enough Machine Time" as Less, Not More

How much product machining is enough? This is one of the most important decisions that you can make. It will affect profit by its impact on product acceptance. It will also affect profit by the way it predetermines whether a product is overengineered and therefore overcosted. Among all the factors that predispose a business to no growth or slow growth, overengineering beyond the point of enough machine time is frequently first and almost always one of the top causes.

The more technical a product is and the more scientific the base from which it originates, the more prevalent overmachining will be.

Machining more performance capability into a product than its market demands and will pay for is the antithesis of managing growth by marketing premium values. Violating the principle of enoughness creates no premium value. It creates, instead, a negative value: more is offered than is needed. This puts a premium on cost in your manufacturing process, not on worth in your customer's use process. Markets pay only to insure their own benefit values as users.

The principle of enoughness is the secret of manufacturing's contribution to your growth. It is fallen short of or exceeded at peril. While the kitchen sink approach to building products appears to reduce risks to growth by throwing in one of everything, it actually increases risk. Just enough, no more and no less no matter what the state of the art, is the first rule of manufacturing for growth.

The sale of products that boast a high machining component is based on show-and-tell. Show the product; tell about its machining. Products whose marketing is well machined never show and tell. They testify to their added benefit value in use and they prove its impact on customer improvement. The only genuine marketing is testify-and-prove. Everything else is product selling.

Manufacturing and engineering are proud sciences. They are proud of their ability to make anything and to make it best. In addition to being proud, they are also dangerous sciences. More often than not, they can indeed make anything and make it best. Unfortunately, what is best in a manufacturing sense is not necessarily best in the perceptions of a market. The machinist's concept of best is best ingredients or components, best processing or construction, and best technical performance. Meanwhile, markets look only for the best benefits.

Machinists make products for the approval and envy of other machinists. Their standards are set by fraternal acceptance. Engineers design for other engineers. After all, who else understands so well the nuances, the subtleties, and the exotica of their technology? Customers, on the other hand, purchase and use for themselves. Made best makes no difference unless it benefits best.

The converse is also true. If a product benefits best, the fact that it is technically less than the best makes no difference.

Product value must be communicated as user value. The value must be more beneficial than alternative values that are available by going to competition or by doing without. As long as a product conveys its market's single most crucial benefit, it is susceptible to fast growth. Without the single most crucial benefit, what else the product has or does not have rarely matters. It will probably not be growable on a fast-track time frame.

Be Sure that Maker's and User's Standards Match

The parable of Lonergan's Leg illustrates the need to focus on user requirements. The perfectly made artificial leg would probably meet two factory standards. First, it would be impervious to the elements and resistant to rust, corrosion, pitting, cracking, crazing, and peeling; it would always look new. Second, it would be strong. Its user could work off the frustration of having to walk with an artificial leg by kicking the side of a locomotive and nothing would happen, at least to the leg. The ideal material to meet these requirements at the factory is stainless steel. But there are few users who would enjoy, let alone prefer, a stainless steel leg.

Manufacturers keep reintroducing Lonergan's Legs in their product lines. Because such products defy their markets' needs, they defy attempts to grow them. Now and again, a market lets a manufacturer know the difference between their two sets of standards before it is too late.

A major paint manufacturer once discovered that batch 2000, which contained a significant deviation from the technical standard, had erroneously passed through the quality control process. A recall campaign was initiated at once, but it was too late. Sales had already been made by the manufacturer's retail outlets. Customers were relentlessly tracked down. Explanations were made, apologies were given, and two cans of another batch were offered in exchange for each imperfect can. Most customers refused. They said it was the best paint they had ever used. Instead of giving it up, they wanted more.

This is an example of backdoor learning. The market is satisfied but the manufacturer is perplexed. Far more common is frontdoor learning where the manufacturer is initially satisfied but the market is eventually dissatisfied. The manufacturer ends up not only perplexed but also deprived of growth.

An electrical products manufacturer set out to create the perfect stepping motor. Three years later he had succeeded. Miniaturized, precisely controllable through each of the 360 degrees of its arc, the motor had only one moving part. High performance and low maintenance would be assured. The motor's small size, controllability, and reliability made it extremely versatile. There would be, its makers forecast, a hundred and one uses for it. There turned out to be none. Everyone acknowledged the motor's benefits. But no one was prepared to accept the unrecoverable costs it would add to the redesign of their equipment or the training costs to teach their engineers how to implement its required new technology. Worst of all, no one wanted to convert design and production processes to accommodate the motor when solid state technology, which seemed to be just around the corner, could make it obsolete.

Some managers like to scorn their markets. Proud of their science, they say, No market ever made a product. This is true. They also say, No market ever proposed a product. This is less true. But markets do one thing that no manufacturer can ever do. *Markets drive products up growth curves.* This is why growth businesses must be driven, in turn, by market needs.

Put Forth Product "Outards"

Why is it a nongrowth strategy to add technical value to a product unless it also adds superior perceived value to its users? Technology has primary worth to technicians. Use benefits have worth to customers and clients. Heavy-profit-contributing users — repetitive large-scale buyers whose purchases yield maximum profit on sales — do not buy product innards. They buy "outards": not what a product is but what it will do for them that they want to have done and can have done as well in no other way.

The more investment capital you pump into innards, the more time you spend in front of your market extolling them without relating them to enhanced user value, the less the likelihood that fast growth will occur.

If users were able to take out of a product on a one-to-one basis what manufacturers put into it, technical value and perceived value would be equal. As it happens, they rarely are. The values that users take out of a product are not technical values but the values added by marketing. Unless an engineered value is marketed so that its single most important benefit is perceived as superior, it will not exist as a buying influence. Instead of contributing to profit on sales, it will make a deadweight contribution to cost.

Product uniqueness, no matter what its quality or how much its quantity, is simply not marketable as such. What, then, is the point of building it into a product in the first place? Engineered value should not be built into a product in the first place; it should wait until the second place. What should precede it? Market research to determine the user values that must be met by a product is what must come first. Then the minimum types and amounts of engineered values needed to deliver the user values can be implemented.

When you use marketing as a growth strategy, it functions like a closed circuit. In your first tour of the circuit, the market makes its initial input value in the form of information. In the second cycle, you supply a product or service output whose added values match up with your information about market needs. In the third cycle, the market makes its second input, this time in units of value called dollars.

Base Marketing Strategy on User Values

Since user values are paramount, what do users value? The answer to this question will provide the content of your marketing strategy.

Specific answers to this question vary from market to market; the general answer remains the same. In one form or another, users seek the maximum increase in their net worth. The act of purchase is an act of acquiring incremental gains. The greater the increment and the greater the propensity to acquire it, the higher the price that customers will be willing to pay for it — and the faster the growth of its marketer.

How do consumer markets express the concept of new worth? In several ways. Time is money. More than that, it is the gift of life itself. Awarding consumers more discretionary time adds to their net worth. Added ease and conveniences do the same. So do added pride, prestige, and pleasure. And so does added money.

Personal balance sheets are no less important to individual consumers than corporate balance sheets are to businessmen. Customers almost always know what adds to their worth and what detracts from it. Even more finitely, they perceive different degrees of increment or decrement from various offers. Marketers are bidders. Many sellers think that all you have to do is scatter an offering and the market will come running. Marketers know that they must do the running, and when they get to market they must also do the bidding. "Buy what I yield" is their cry: not buy my product but buy the best available increase in your net worth.

Mobilize Added Values Three Ways

What does it really mean to offer a customer added value? It means that you are giving him new options for the use of his money. You are not just opening up new sources of revenue for him. You are broadening his options for capital management.

What will he do with the money you give him? Like all business managers, he has two basic options.

First, he can choose to distribute some or all of the new money as dividends to shareholders. Why? To help him protect his present source of capital and insure it as a future source.

Or he can choose to invest some or all of the new money in plant, equipment, or operations. Why? To grow his capital base.

What will be the outcome from exercising these options? As a result of your marketing strategy, customer companies will be able to grow their profits faster. Think of it this way: Your own fast-growth marketing strategy must be designed to help your customers grow faster too. Fast growth creates fast growth.

Of all the characteristics that you as a seller and your customers can share, can you imagine a more binding way to cement your relationship than to help each other to grow faster?

OFFER USERS A NEW OPPORTUNITY

The marketable benefit of adding to the net worth of an industrial customer or a professional service client is not the new money itself. It is what can be done with the money. It is, in short, a new *opportunity.*

The opportunity may be to make a newly affordable investment. It may be to add to an existing one. It may be to add to savings. It may be to divest or disinvest out of an inferior commitment in favor of a replacement source of funds that can promise a superior return. Whatever the exact nature of the opportunity, it represents in one form or another *the chance to acquire new money.* It is dollars and cents that are being transacted, not product ingredients, components, or the performance characteristics they make possible.

What sort of deals leading to fast growth can you enter into with users in search of added opportunity value? Your role is to hold out the value. Allege its superiority; that is, claim for it the capability of delivering the prime available opportunity to acquire new money. If it is a premium opportunity, it can command a premium price.

With industrial customers and professional service clients, the incremental net value to be marketed can often be precisely calculated and concisely stated. In these markets, use values exist as tangible, quantifiable sums. Adding value means one of two benefits. The sum will be enlarged by a significant new revenue source. Or the existing sum will be preserved by saving or reducing devaluation caused by an otherwise inevitable cost.

The end result is that more dollars remain in or flow into the user's pot. If these added dollars flow from your ability to increase a customer's sales revenues, they will take on a unique charm. What is it? Simply, this: Profits on a customer's incremental volume can be significantly higher than profits on his existing volume. Why is this so? Most businesses have underutilized capacity to manufacture and sell. Their ability to make and sell exceeds the demand. Incremental sales volume may not add at all to overhead. Or it may not add to overhead to a degree commensurate with its return. The new variable costs incurred by incremental sales may be relatively unoppressive. In the short run, just as fixed costs tend to remain fixed, even variable costs may not vary much. The same sales manager can supervise the incremental sales. The investment in his overhead need not increase. The size of the sales force need not increase. And so on.

As long as existing capabilities can be used, or mostly used, the profit margins on extra units of a customer's sales are always capable of being higher. This fact is a secret of growth. *Incremental profits are the growth profits.*

In this kind of transaction, the price that a user is asked to pay enjoys a unique distinction. In the traditional sense, every price represents a cost. Yet here, price is an investment. The difference comes about because it will yield a quantifiable return. If the value-to-price relationship of a brand is maintained, the value of the return will exceed the price of the investment. A positive return will be achievable by the user even though you charge him a premium price.

The role of marketing in fast growth can now be clearly seen. *Marketing is a brand's investment proposal.* It sets up the deal. The technology of making investment proposals is the essential skill of business growth. Without it, even the most superior machinist can never position his product as an investment opportunity.

REGARD CUSTOMERS AS INVESTORS

What is the advantage of regarding your heavy-profit-contributing customers as investors, your brand's end use as delivering a prime opportunity for them to add new money to their personal or professional bottom lines, and the purpose of your marketing function as proposing that they gain the new money by investing with you? There are several superficial answers and a single genuine one. You can gain customers, improve share of market, and increase sales volume. But none of these is your principal objective. The one genuine advantage is that your inflow of growth profits will increase on the basis of your ability to command a premium price.

MAKE PREMIUM PRICE A BARGAIN

Marketing is designed to do more than justify the premium price it calls for. Justification is a defensive maneuver. Brand marketing is assertive. It makes your price, even at a premium level, appear to be a bargain by comparing it favorably with its return. Price and its return should not be excessively far apart. This permits price to be perceived in relationship to the return it will provide. If the price is high and yet the return exceeds it, the basis for a deal exists.

What is the proper relationship between investment and yield? Which is the cause and which is the effect? From a rational, real-world standpoint, an investment is the cause of its yield. But in brand marketing it is the other way around. The yield that is being proposed is the cause of the customer's investment that is being solicited. If there were no yield, there would be no investment. If there is no premium yield, there will be no premium investment. On a supply-and-demand basis, the yield being supplied creates the demand. This is how marketing generates sales.

Product selling and the marketing of an investment opportunity are two entirely different operations. The formula for a product sale can be represented like this:

Product features = Product benefits at a fair price

Selling product is a no-growth or slow-growth occupation. Fair price is apt to be fairer to the buyer than to the seller. It is profit-deprived. Its margins are preshrunk by competitive bidding and by the high cost of sale required to negotiate price based on smaller and smaller differences between rival benefits.

Growth profits can come only from applying the marketing formula:

Premium perceived value > Premium price

To put it colloquially from the user's point of view, markets are invited by marketing to spend money to make money. This is the way customers and clients get rich; marketers too. Both work on the same principle. To make money, you must invest money. Only money makes money. Marketing is the proposer of increased capital growth for you and your customers.

If your marketing carries out this function, you will be branded by your markets as a grower of their businesses. In turn, they will help you grow your own. No other business function can give you, or them, this leverage on growth.

8

Dominate Your Category Preemptively — Not as a Competitor

If there is a secret to fast growth, it is this: Establish a transient monopoly and maintain it as long as you can. Monopoly profits are premium profits and premium profits are the source of fast growth.

How can you maintain a monopoly legally? There is only one way. Monopolize the preference of your heavy-profit-contributing markets by preempting their need for a source of their single most crucial benefit.

Preferential monopoly is market-derived, not manufacturer-derived. It is the only monopoly that can be enforced because markets themselves enforce it by their purchase behavior. It is not really your product they will want. Nor is it preference for you as a supplier they will be displaying. It will be an insistence on obtaining your product benefit, which in their perception is the single best.

Dominate by Taking Profit Leadership

Preemption of market preference is the way to create dominance in your product category. To be dominant as a fast-growth business, you do not have to be the sales leader. Nor are you required to possess the leading market share. You may own volume and share supremacy as a coincidence, but you do not have to. What you must achieve is profit leadership in terms of profit on sales.

Leadership in profit on sales is the acid test of market preference. It validates the market's value-to-price perception of your product by proving that premium value merits a premium price. By doing so, it correlates a customer's willingness to believe in your product's high worth with his or her willingness to budget for a high margin on its price. Belief that is professed but is not accompanied by budgeting for high margin purchases is balderdash.

When, as, and if you can achieve dominance of your product category, you will come to have three significant advantages whose return on your investment in dominance can be vital. First, you will discourage competition. Transient monopoly tends to perpetuate its state of transience. Second, you will force competitors to adopt a reactive strategy to you. Reactive strategies are often predictable. They are also easier to defend against. Third, competitors will have to ferret out thin vertical segments of your market in order to gain a toehold. Microminiature segmentation is always costly and may not always be profitable.

As the dominant factor in your market, you have two things going for you. Cash flow is strong and dependable, so your profits will provide the money to play the marketing game. Market acceptance is also strong, so you will be in the best possible position to discourage competition. You can lock onto the core group of heavy profit contributors. You can also protect yourself against the fractional impacts of vertical segmentation from covetous rivals.

When IBM was at the height of its dominance in a wide range of data processing markets, no would-be competitor dared to take it on frontally. In fact, most potential rivals had an inviolable rule to avoid entry into any market where IBM straddled preference of the core group of heavy profit contributors. Procter & Gamble is another company that has commanded this same respect. Both organizations believe that the best competitor is one who opens a new market segment, not one who takes them on head to head in their own segments.

Outfox the Comparable Competitor

Dominance occurs when two preceding conditions are met. One is that customer or consumer awareness must be superior in regard to you as supplier and to your product as delivering the best benefit. The second is that user attitudes toward you as supplier and your product benefit must be superior. When these two situations prevail, it is easy but mistaken to believe that you own a market. Quite the contrary, you have permitted a market to own you as the favored supplier and to own your product benefit. This, more than any other reason, is why transient monopolies persist. A market will simply not let go of a preferred benefit and a favored supplier.

Competition, however, is not apt to be so kind. Its thrust is to retard your speed of growth, stabilize it, and turn it downward. It attacks your rate of growth first and then the direction of your growth curve. How does it do this? Competitors go after your dominance in a market and try to atomize it. They seek to destroy the monolithic preference your customers hold for you by picking off a share of preference for themselves. They target on grabbing a piece of market awareness and converting it to themselves as suppliers of the best benefit. They attempt to focus some of the market's positive attitudes on their own benefits.

The net effect of competition is to demand that your market compare. To make you comparable is to de-position you as incomparable; that is, as being branded. For this reason, you must not practice dominance as a competitor. You can achieve it preemptively only in a market situation where there are no truly comparable competitors. In order to achieve dominance, two questions have to be answered. What must be preempted? How?

Bring Dominance to Your Users, Not Products

If you are going to become the dominant brand in your product or service category, you will have to forsake the natural temptation to go before your customers and proclaim to them that you are best: your product, your service, or your benefits. Trying to make your product dominant by exaltation will not work. Neither will demonstration. It is the user, not the product, whom you must make dominant.

Customer enhancement, not product performance, must be preempted as the requisite to dominance. You cannot say, we are best, and expect to dominate—even if you are. You must be able to say to the customer, You will be best when you do business with us. You will obtain the best nourishment and have the best health. You will be the most attractive or the most capable or the best off after retirement. You will have the best profit or the best profit most consistently. Do not claim to be *better,* which is comparative and invites competitive comparison. Claim to be the *best,* which is superlative and preempts competition.

Dominant users—customers who have been made to feel dominant by you—are the backbone of your growth. They are the customers who have a personal stake in your business. If they are to continue their dominance, they know that you must continue to prosper and grow. They are your self-interested supporters, your ultimate financiers, and in a very real sense your partners in growth. They are unusually good partners. They pay their own way. They pay your way too.

You depend on your dominant users for business continuity; they depend on you for continuing their dominance. You depend on them for adding value to your business; they depend on you for adding value to them, their lives, or their businesses. Growth is a symbiotic process between the grower and the grown. Each of you serves as both for the other.

Maximize the Marketing Contribution

The role of marketing can be defined in relation to dominance. It is to put benefit pressure on a market, to adjust the pressure gradient to the most cost-effective level, and to take the air out of the counterpressures of competitive benefits. How can marketing, defined in this manner, contribute to dominance? There are three ways: benefit singleness, ceaselessness of repetition, and distribution narrowness of your marketing drive.

Benefit singleness. Dominance is most frequently a direct result of selecting a market's single most crucial benefit and marketing it. Benefit singleness is essential. As a rule, customers have little need or ability to apply several benefits and less inclination to recall them. Multiple benefits fall of their own weight.

While there may be no one reason why all heavy profit contributors in a core market will prefer your product, there is usually one single most crucial benefit they will all be able to mobilize around with closely similar degrees of passion. Sometimes the single crucial benefit will be their sole area of concurrence. At other times it will be their major area of passionate concurrence. If you are lucky, you will be able to come up with a single crucial benefit that will have a ripple effect: that is, it will be able to suggest by inference one or more linked benefits.

By putting forward a single benefit, and always putting it forward in exactly the same form and style, you can capitalize on its premium for high memorability and highly accurate association with your business and attribution to your product. You provide your product with a synonym: what it *does,* which serves as a parallel name for what it *is.* Product name and benefit theme become one and the same, interrelated and interchangeable.

Ceaselessness of repetition. Repetition has long been said to be the mother of knowledge. There is a very good chance that it is also the mother of dominance.

A single most crucial benefit lends itself admirably to repetition. Its simplicity and concentration make the message economical. This allows marketing resources to be conserved. They can be concentrated for investment in the media which will provide enough repetition to insure maximum impact on customer awareness and attitudes. Repetition, the more the better, is the multiplier of the benefit message. It is also a source of its perceived credibility.

Messages seen and heard often are messages believed. Perhaps that statement should be amended: True messages that are seen and heard frequently in honorable contexts are messages believed. But no matter how many qualifications are added, messages rarely seen or heard are less believable than those whose frequency is great. How great must repetitive frequency be? At least one time more than you are prepared to accept. A good rule of thumb to remember is that when you are wearying of your product benefit's ceaseless repetition, the market is probably just beginning to perceive it. When you can stand it no longer, the market is just coming to understand it. When you want to change the message or reduce its frequency, it is just beginning to exert benefit pressure on the market.

Distribution narrowness. A ceaselessly repeated single benefit must be beamed to its core market with laserlike intensity if it is to activate the people you want to make dominant, your heavy profit contributors. The temptation to tell everybody everything every time is something you will have to overcome if effectiveness is going to be a handmaiden to your growth.

As with all businesses, turnover is a key to your fast growth. Turning over a relatively small market constituency at an accelerated rate is part of the formula for growing a business faster than average. Because your heavy profit contributors undoubtedly compose a relatively small number of all your customers, they are susceptible to rapid turn if you zero in on them narrowly with your message and do not diffuse it too broadly beyond their bounds. To the same extent that concentration favors turnover, diffusion defeats dominance.

As a direct result of defining your message distribution narrowly, you may have to be prepared to allocate a high up-front investment to move each heavy profit contributor or heavy-profit-contributing prospect. It is a fair tradeoff for his or her premium-price purchase from you. Superior purchase value merits superior promotional value. Do not be misled by common indexes of distribution cost-benefit analysis. Beware especially of cost-per-thousand. Always ask, cost-per-thousand *what?* If the answer is heavy profit contributors, stay and investigate. They are your source of dominance. If the answer is customers and prospects in general, run.

Make Sure Your Three Productivities Are High

When you come right down to it, dominance is a matter of establishing and maintaining unusually high productivity in three management areas under your influence: your own labor force, your distribution, and your customers.

Labor force productivity. Your labor productivity—a concept you should interpret broadly to include your managers as well as your workforce—is the product of total dollar sales divided by the total man-hours you require to generate them. If you want to dominate your category, you will need a high level of productivity to keep your cost curve down so you can assure low-cost supply. Labor productivity is also important in assuring that you can guarantee full channel availability for your product throughout its distribution chain on a cost-effective basis.

If your labor productivity is low, you will be a high-cost producer. You can look at that fact in two ways. You will be spending a lot to produce a little. Or you will be producing a little that costs a lot. Either way, you will have to deal with the problems of profit absorption by costs or insufficient distribution.

When you can produce only a little that costs a lot, you risk becoming back-ordered and out of stock. This is the equivalent of defeating your fast-growth objectives by acting as your own competitor. Not only are you precluded from selling. You are also inviting your committed and potential customers to sample competitive offerings. If they find the experience to be better than their experience with you, or even if they find it to be merely equal, they may become a competitor's heavy profit contributors. It will cost you dear in time and dollars to win them back, assuming you can succeed at all.

The real cost of suboptimal labor productivity may not be higher production costs, although they will occur. It may not even be the opportunity loss of cost-effective distribution. The true cost may be the loss of future sales from your existing heavy profit contributors—the very antithesis of fast growth.

Distribution productivity. Your distribution productivity is the product of total dollar sales per square foot of inventory or display space on the shelves of your retailers, dealers, or distributors.

To grow fast, you need to maximize turnover velocity. At distribution, shelf space is regarded as the source of profit. The more dollars each square foot produces, the greater the profit it will contribute.

Physical distribution is one of your customer markets. If you cannot sell to distribution, everything else is academic. Channels are never in your hands. As with all customers, they can only be cajoled and never controlled. You are in their hands. Whether they handle you in ways that maximize your growth rate or minimize it depends on how well you teach them how to sell for you. To get on their shelves is only the minor part of the solution. To help them get your product off their shelves is the major part, for this is the key to their contribution to your dominance.

Your distribution market segment is your teaching segment. What does teaching your distributors consist of? It means teaching them how to sell by teaching their own customers how to apply your product to their needs: in short, teaching them how to teach. Distributors teach your products off their shelves and into the market. You are directly dependent on their teaching skills for distribution productivity. Your costs of distribution, therefore, should be heavily weighted with teaching costs.

If you are importantly dependent on distribution, you will need to be in a second business parallel to your product or service business. The second business will be a school for your distributors, an educational organization and curriculum of some kind that will be devoted to what the French call *vitesse*: speeded movement that intensifies your productivity.

Customer productivity. Your customer productivity is the product of the profit value contributed by each sales transaction. Dominance in your market depends on the combination of a high profit percentage on sales along with at least reasonably high sales turnover. As a branded supplier, your ability to command a premium price should insure your margin. If you can solve the riddle of repeat or big-ticket sales, you will be able to enlist the productivity of your customers in your pursuit of fast growth.

Customer productivity tends to be high in certain types of businesses. One high-productivity business is a systems business. A system can earn a premium profit because the profit on the whole can be greater than the profit on the system's individual parts. The value added by collating the system, integrating it as a related unit, and applying it as a multiple problem solver in a customer's business adds value to its margin. Worth more, it can demand more.

Another type of high-productivity business is based on the strategy of razor and blades. The razor component is a durable. It is almost always a commodity. Hence, it usually carries a low margin. The blades are consumables. They are the profit makers. Their unit margin can be high because they are generally branded with a unique benefit. Their volume will also be high. This is an infallible recipe for fast growth.

Razor strategy is emplacement. Any margin above breakeven will suffice to put a razor in place. Blade strategy is turnover. The higher the margin and the faster the turn, the better the profit. Razor blades themselves are the best example of this strategy. So are ballpoint pen refills, camera film, computer printout paper, and abrasives for metal-cleaning machinery. Services can also act as blades, bringing a customer back again and again into a purchase cycle.

The quest for customers—getting them—always seems to be the most difficult task in managing a business for fast growth. Yet it rarely turns out that way. Getting customers is a cost. If you are willing to pay your dues, you can get customers—once. Turning them and returning them to your business is where profit is made. The faster you bring them back and the more profit they contribute to you on each return, the faster you will grow.

What is it that keeps bringing customers back? Nothing less than the perception that they can achieve or maintain their dominance only by doing business with you. If you have a business objective, this should be it.

Be Vigilant Against the Dissolution of Dominance

When dominance dissipates, it goes a little at a time at first. Its initial slippage may be very slight. It does not always start with a downturn. Your rate of growth may simply level off. This is a warning sign; take it seriously. You will be tempted to rationalize it away as a temporary aberration—a natural consequence of nonrecurring factors beyond your control. More than likely, this peculiar combination of factors has never happened before. In all probability it will never come about again. There is nothing wrong, you will insist, with the inherent soundness of the business. You may be right. But the odds are greater that the market is trying to tell you something.

Pride may or may not go before a fall. But pride will most assuredly prevent you from perceiving a fall for what it is.

Any slowdown in the rate of growth of a fast-growing business must be taken to heart. A business that is still growing but is growing slower is no longer a fast-growth business—a growth business, yes, but not a fast-growth business. Why has its thrust subsided? You must find out. You will probably not have to look everywhere. Almost always, the answer will be found in market preference. Your heavy profit contributors will have stopped preferring your benefit as the best. Their repeat purchase rate will have diminished. The entry of new heavy profit contributors into first purchase will have tailed off. Loss of growth thrust is almost always the early warning signal of a demand curve that has begun to run out of steam.

The more time you spend looking for reasonable excuses, the less time you will have left for remedial action. Time is of the essence. The slower your rate of growth becomes, the longer it will usually take to bring it back to speed. In growing a business, longer equals costlier. If you wait too long—and this may not be very long at all in a real time sense—you may find it impossible to turn the curve around.

If it is to be repaired, a growth dropoff must be treated as a short-term problem. Do not wait for next quarter's confirmation over and over again. Give up the belief, before it takes you over, that you can make up one quarter's inactivity by spending just a little more money later. Slow growth and no growth are insidious. Once they settle in, they alter the complexion of a business. They force it off its growth plan. They dissolve its dominance. They transform it into a mature stable business whose objective is to maintain its market. Or, even worse, they convert it into a mature declining business whose objective is to regain market share or stave off further decline as long as possible.

When rate of growth winds down, maturity sets in. The business has settled out. It has found its peak. The investment community, your shareholders, competitors, the trade, and your market will curse you with this image. Your price command will weaken, then vanish. Your branded status will disappear. Your product line will become a commodity, marked by competitive comparison and marked down by price sensitivity.

How can you maintain vigilance against loss of dominance? The first strategy is to monitor your rate of growth on a continuing basis. Increase your marketing pressure or alter its mix immediately when you see a lag. Increasing pressure is a good second strategy. It requires the least change. If results are not forthcoming quickly, you can start experimenting with your marketing mix. Change the variables one at a time or in systems: advertising alone, for example, or advertising and sales in combination; sales contacts and calls alone or sales and increased distribution in combination. This will give you a third strategy.

If laggard growth is not susceptible to marketing rejuvenation, you may have a product problem. Have your use benefits been obsoleted by competitive technology? Has your value-to-price ratio been exceeded by rival values? When you consider cost-effectiveness, do you find that your product applications have become more costly or less effective? If you answer yes, you will have to go back to the drawing board.

What if fast growth cannot be regained? The ideal solution is to have a new fast-growth business up your sleeve that will start a new curve and give you a new chance to take a market of heavy profit contributors into the dominance of a major aspect of their personal or professional lives.

PART IV

The Four Fast-Growth Organizing and Operating Strategies

9

Enlist Top Managers' Support — Tell Them What You Need

How can your top managers dedicate your company as a growth medium: to attract and retain fast-growth managers who can throw off businesses that grow at twice or more the rate of the gross national product?

Believing as we do that in the business of the 1980s, either we learn how to grow fast or we will be caught, we are convinced that dedicating your company to growth cannot be left to chance. Do not wait for your top managers to establish a learning curve. Help them adapt their organization and operations to become more supportive to entrepreneurial managers. Talk to them something like this.

A fast-growth business must be run as a teaching business and as a service business for its corporateurs. It must teach them the principles of growing a business fast. It must repeat these principles over and over again so that they cannot be forgotten. Eventually, they will become its gospel. The corporation preaches it. Its corporateurs practice it.

The practice of growth strategies must be supported by corporate services: by market information services that probe market needs, segment them, and assay the profit from serving them; by financial services that calculate volume-cost-profit ratios, pricing parameters, and the improved profits that can accrue to customers if a business is mounted to serve them; by technical services, customer application services, promotional services, management consultation services to keep corporateurs on track and out of trouble—services that help fast-growth managers grow fast.

In a world where there are no free lunches, where does the money come from to pay for these teaching and service investments? The corporateurs who use them pay for them out of their fast-grown profits. First they make money. Then their money makes money by being plowed back into support for their next money-making thrusts. This is the self-regenerating cycle of fast-growth management.

Along with teaching and service supports, three additional ways of organizing and operating are necessary to turn a company into a growth medium. They have to do with staff teams, small entities, and rewards for the corporateurs.

STAFF SUPPORT TEAMS

In order to grow their businesses, fast-growth managers must practice functional concentration. Marketing will be their chief function. Other functions will be deemphasized by corporateurs. The other functions retain their importance but lose their priority for the corporateur. How will they be handled? The best way is to set up support service teams to execute these functions for their corporate entrepreneurs.

Consolidated staff teams are not new. They have been at work inside many large companies for years. A few of them, such as in-house communications groups and education functions, have even been spun out by their parent companies as more or less autonomous subsidiaries.

Support teams are best put together on a modular basis, with modules being added or dropped off as the needs of fast-growth managers require. This policy helps service teams avoid the costs and operational dead weight of nonessential staff. It also follows the principle of concentration.

Most teams contain three resources: financial, manufacturing, and market analysis. When a corporateur is heavily involved in new product marketing or new market entry, which are two of the most formidable growth assignments, additional modular services from inside and outside the company can be attached to a support team in a consultative role. Every staff team member is expected to be a professional performer in his or her function. This enables each specialist to provide experience and expertise in an area of supportive knowledge where a corporateur must make cost-effective decisions.

SMALL-ENTITY BUILDING

Corporate managers work best within compact business entities. Compact doesn't necessarily mean tiny; it means that an entity must be small enough to be managed entrepreneurially. A small entity should be a single business, not a miniconglomerate composed of several product lines which serve several diverse markets. A one-on-one relationship between a product line and its market is ideal.

Smallness of size also enables a manager to encompass a business unit emotionally as well as operationally. Emotional involvement is critical to growth. Smith must be able to think of his business — and should be encouraged by top management to think of it — as "Smith's business." Brown must be able to think of her business as "Brown's business." Another justification for small-entity creation is that it makes easier the corporateur's practice of directive leadership and the practice of giving budgets to people rather than to faceless functions.

Like consolidated staff teams, small business entities are not new either. In various forms, such as task teams, venture groups, and project squads, they have demonstrated that they encourage innovation. At the same time, they reduce some of the typical cost-ineffectiveness of innovation by enabling their managers to keep a close watch on profits and how they are being made or frittered away. In the form of minicompanies or "corporettes," they retain these advantages.

INCENTIVE REWARD SYSTEM

Money rewards are the major incentives for many fast-growth managers. As they perceive money, it acts as compensation for their risk taking. It also helps them quantify their accomplishment.

To attract and motivate the movers of business growth, incentive systems must be put in place that frankly acknowledge superior money payout as their primary benefit. A salary and bonus package can contain several options: bonus as a standard percentage of growth profit achievement, which has the effect of a royalty; profit sharing on a rising sliding scale; or an equity allotment in real or phantom stock. Whatever the incentive sweetener, the central point for management to remember is that no manager will grow someone else's business to its utmost on a salary reward alone.

If your company authorizes staff support teams for its corporateurs, builds small entities for them to manage for fast growth, and rewards them lucratively, will these three acts do the job of converting the company into a growth medium? Almost, but not quite. One further characteristic is really needed: Top management must be obsessed with growing at least some of its businesses with a higher than average velocity. This magnificent obsession must occupy one of the loftiest priorities in its hierarchy of values. It must be a constant devotion. It must be transparent.

As with all philosophies of business management, growth dedication must start at the top or it will never start at all.

Index